200 NiGHTTiME PRAYERS FOR Teen Girls

Words of Comfort for a
Sweet, Peaceful Sleep

When you lie down,
you will not be afraid;
when you lie down,
your sleep will be sweet.

PROVERBS 3:24 NIV

HILARY BERNSTEIN

200 NighTTime PRAYERS FOR Teen Girls

Words of Comfort for a Sweet, Peaceful Sleep

BARBOUR BOOKS
An Imprint of Barbour Publishing, Inc.

Lula,
Happy Sweet 16th Birthday!
You have grown into
a beautifull young lady..
inside and out. Enjoy
this special day and this
book.
Love Always,
Bubbe & Papa
1/28/2023

Published by Barbour Books, an imprint of Barbour Publishing, Inc., 1810 Barbour Drive, Uhrichsville, Ohio 44683, www.barbourbooks.com

Our mission is to inspire the world with the life-changing message of the Bible.

Member of the
Evangelical Christian
Publishers Association

Printed in China.

INTRODUCTION

If ever there was a time of needing sweet sleep, it's now. Every day, things scream for your attention: friends, school, family, social media, chores, activities, relationships, emotions. . .the list goes on. It's easy to get distracted from what really matters. Those distractions have a way of wearing you out and stealing your peace and joy so it's hard to fall asleep at night.

Life's busyness and distractions don't just threaten to rob your sleep, they make it harder to get close to Your heavenly Father too. Yet He's the One who longs to bring you peace. He's the One who will make your sleep sweet.

Being a teen isn't easy. During this time when everything in your life seems so topsy-turvy and uncertain, my prayer is that you'll use this book to quiet yourself and refocus on our Lord and His Word. I've jam-packed it with truth that will quiet your heart, fill you with peace, and bring restful nights of sweet sleep.

Sweet dreams!
Hilary Bernstein

JESUS LOVES ME

I pray that you, being rooted and established in love, may have power, together with all the Lord's holy people, to grasp how wide and long and high and deep is the love of Christ, and to know this love that surpasses knowledge—that you may be filled to the measure of all the fullness of God.

EPHESIANS 3:17–19 NIV

Father God, Your love is amazing. And Jesus' love for me is beyond what I can even wrap my brain around. Jesus loves me. Me! I don't need to do anything on my own to earn that love. All I need is to believe in Him and accept His love as a beautiful gift. Day by day, moment by moment, please give me power to begin to grasp how wide and long and high and deep Christ's love is for me. It's a marvelous thing that can transform every part of my life. In Jesus' name I pray, amen.

STOP STRIVING

"Be still, and know that I am God."

PSALM 46:10 ESV

Father, I come to You weighed down by my busyness. So much is going on in my life, and I feel like I'm cramming so much into my days. I know I don't have to do all the things to make You love me. In fact, Your Word tells me to be still and know You are God. That means I need to stop striving. I admit it feels almost impossible to be still. It's hard to not strive, and it feels like everything in this world is so far from being still. Yet tonight, as I draw close to You, I choose to quiet my heart. I want to take this time to be still with You. In this quiet place, please help me to know You are God. In Jesus' name I pray, amen.

NO WORRIES

Humble yourselves, therefore, under
God's mighty hand, that he may lift you
up in due time. Cast all your anxiety
on him because he cares for you.

1 PETER 5:6–7 NIV

Father, knowing that You care for me changes my life. I'm so glad You love me and that I matter to You. And I'm so thankful I can tell You all of my cares and worries. I know You'll listen to me and help. So many things feel like burdens right now. They're weighing me down. But I choose to surrender them to You. I know I can't handle all that I'm facing and feeling, but I know You can. You're mighty enough to do more than I can even imagine. I trust You'll work out all the details. When I'm tempted to feel anxious, please replace all of my worry with peace. Please help me trust You completely and rest in that trust. In Jesus' name I pray, amen.

MORE THAN SKIN-DEEP

But the LORD said to Samuel, "Do not
consider his appearance or his height,
for I have rejected him. The LORD does
not look at the things people look at.
People look at the outward appearance,
but the LORD looks at the heart."

1 SAMUEL 16:7 NIV

Father God, I admit it's hard to not focus on appearances. It feels natural to judge my looks. I don't always like what I see, even though You created me and You see what's inside of me. It's also really hard to not judge other people by what they look like. I know I shouldn't, but I do. Please help me see what's really inside others so I can make wise choices about my friends. Please open my eyes to see people who need You—and help me to reach out to them, especially if I normally wouldn't want to talk with them. Please help me look deeper than just the surface level. In Jesus' name I pray, amen.

TOMORROW

Yet you do not know what your life will be like tomorrow. You are just a vapor that appears for a little while and then vanishes away.

JAMES 4:14 NASB

Lord, it's hard for me to remember that the worries and troubles of today won't last forever. I don't know what tomorrow will hold. I kind of wish I did. But I'm choosing to trust You. And as much as I wonder what will happen tomorrow—or next week or next month or next year—I don't have to worry. I know You're in control, and You have a wonderful plan. Even if it doesn't always feel like it, life is so short. Please help me make the most of every day. Especially my not-so-great days! Instead of getting discouraged or frustrated when things don't go my way, please help me to see You at work and trust You more and more. In Jesus' name I pray, amen.

SPEAK UP!

Speak up for those who cannot speak for themselves, for the rights of all who are destitute. Speak up and judge fairly; defend the rights of the poor and needy.

PROVERBS 31:8–9 NIV

Father God, thank You for giving me a voice! You've given me thoughts and words not only to express my feelings but also to speak up for others. Please use me to help other people, even if it seems awkward or uncomfortable. Please work on my heart so I have more compassion for people around me. Open my eyes so I can see who needs help. I want to do what's right and defend people who have a hard time defending themselves. I pray I'll be a kind friend to other teens who are left out. Please help me include outsiders and treat everyone with kindness, no matter what they look like, sound like, or what they can or cannot do. I'm trusting that You'll use me in a big way in someone else's life. In Jesus' name I pray, amen.

MY MOUTH AND MY HEART

*If you confess with your mouth Jesus as Lord,
and believe in your heart that God raised Him
from the dead, you will be saved; for with
the heart a person believes, resulting in
righteousness, and with the mouth
he confesses, resulting in salvation.*

ROMANS 10:9-10 NASB

Jesus, I do confess that You are Lord! And I truly believe in my heart of hearts that God raised You from the dead and that You're living right now. Thank You that You save me when I confess in faith that You're my Lord. And thank You that as I believe in You, You make me right with You. Being saved and being made right—salvation and righteousness—are such huge things I could never accomplish on my own. Thank You for taking care of both of them for me and choosing to give both salvation and righteousness to me. You are so very good! In Your name I pray, amen.

A LIFE OF KINDNESS

Whoever pursues righteousness and kindness
will find life, righteousness, and honor.
PROVERBS 21:21 ESV

Heavenly Father, it's so interesting that, just like believers should be known for their love, if I pursue kindness—a very loving trait—I'll find life. I pray that I'll seek and find a life of love and kindness. I want to be right in Your eyes. And I want to bring kindness to others. I'm definitely happy to find righteousness and honor along the way. But instead of only focusing on those rewards, I'd really rather concentrate on living a life that pleases You and blesses the people You bring across my daily path. I admit that some days I'd rather not be very righteous or kind at all. But deep down, I want to do all these things for Your glory, Lord! In Jesus' name I pray, amen.

SAFE AND PROTECTED

I love you, O LORD, my strength. The LORD is my rock and my fortress and my deliverer, my God, my rock, in whom I take refuge, my shield, and the horn of my salvation, my stronghold. I call upon the LORD, who is worthy to be praised, and I am saved from my enemies.

PSALM 18:1–3 ESV

O Lord, I do love You! It's such a relief to know that You are my strength, my rock, my fortress. When I'm in trouble, You'll help me. Even when it's obvious that I have enemies—whether bullies verbally or physically threaten me—I know You'll save me. You're my protector, and for that I praise You! I'm thankful I can completely put my trust in You and call upon You at any time. As I fall asleep tonight, I pray I can rest peacefully, knowing that You care about me and protect me moment by moment. In Jesus' name I pray, amen.

A GOOD WORK

For I am confident of this very thing,
that He who began a good work in you will
perfect it until the day of Christ Jesus.

PHILIPPIANS 1:6 NASB

Father, sometimes I look at my life and it doesn't feel like there are many good things in it. My relationships are confusing. Life feels like a mess and so unlike the way I wish it was. But I absolutely trust You and am overwhelmed by the fact that You've begun a good work in me. In me! And by faith, I know You'll finish that good work until it's complete. I don't have to worry about perfecting what You're doing because You're the One who began the work and will continue perfecting it. Please help me to not get in Your way. Please open my eyes so I can see some of the good works You're accomplishing in me and through me. In Jesus' name I pray, amen.

PLEASE FORGIVE ME

I do not understand what I do. For what
I want to do I do not do, but what I hate I do.
ROMANS 7:15 NIV

Father, I have sinned against You today—and I really, really regret it. I wish I weren't so quick to sin. I wish I could obey You, and I wish I could make good decisions. Tomorrow, please help me honor You moment by moment in what I think, say, and do. Please help me live a righteous life—not in a holier-than-thou, judgmental sort of way toward my friends and family. But in the hidden places of my heart, please help me live the kind of life that reflects You as my Lord. I want to be authentic and live for You, not for myself. In Jesus' name I pray, amen.

BELIEVE AND LOVE

*This is his command: to believe in the name
of his Son, Jesus Christ, and to love one another
as he commanded us. The one who keeps
God's commands lives in him, and he in them.
And this is how we know that he lives in us:
We know it by the Spirit he gave us.*

1 JOHN 3:23–24 NIV

Lord Jesus, I believe in Your name, and I want to do what You've commanded. I pray Your Spirit will clearly direct me and help me live out Your commands in everyday life. You lived a life of love; I want to do the same, even if and when it's not easy. Please help Your love be obvious in my life and in the way I treat everyone around me. Even when I need to deal with the unlovable or people who are downright mean, please help me choose to love them. Thank You for Your love and for the way it completely changed my life and future. Thank You also for Your Spirit and for the way He is proof that You live in me. In Your name I pray, amen.

IN GOD I TRUST

*Some trust in chariots and some in horses,
but we trust in the name of the LORD our God.*
PSALM 20:7 ESV

Father God, when I look around me every day, I see people trusting in all sorts of things—money, power, grades, friends, clothing, social media likes, and themselves. But why trust in any of that? What can those things do? If they aren't fleeting—and so many of them are—they're powerless. I don't want to trust in the things of this world. I don't want to get caught up in obsessing over something that's just temporary. And I certainly don't want to trust in myself. But I trust You. I trust that You have all power and authority. I pray I'll continue to rest in You when I'm tempted to shift my eyes and attention on myself or on trivial things. Thank You that You're trustworthy! In Jesus' name I pray, amen.

HERE I AM!

Then I heard the voice of the Lord saying,
"Whom shall I send? And who will go for us?"
And I said, "Here am I. Send me!"

ISAIAH 6:8 NIV

Father, You are awesome. Before anything was, You were. You spoke absolutely everything into existence. And You had and still have a plan for everything and everyone. Even me. Sometimes I wonder if You can ever use me to do Your work or do great things for You. But as long as I listen to Your direction, obey, and do Your work, You can and will use me. That's amazing! I pray You'll give me strength and courage to step out and do Your work. When there's fear in my heart, please give me courage. When I doubt what I should do, please give me clarity. When I'm tempted to stick to what's comfortable, please help me choose obedience over all. Here I am. Send me. In Jesus' name I pray, amen.

No Drifting

We must pay the most careful attention,
therefore, to what we have heard,
so that we do not drift away.

HEBREWS 2:1 NIV

Father God, I'm so glad I've heard Your truth. Not only have I heard it, but I fully believe it and want to be obedient to You and Your Word. I want to follow You. I don't want to drift away. Even when I feel pushed and pulled to be more like the world, I want to be more like You. I don't want to fall into the trap of doing things to fit in with my friends. And I don't want to do what's popular if it doesn't line up with Your truth. Please help me bravely live for You. Keep me close to You, and show me what Your good, pleasing, and perfect will is for my life. In Jesus' name I pray, amen.

ALL MY HEART

Trust in the LORD with all your heart and
do not lean on your own understanding.
In all your ways acknowledge Him,
and He will make your paths straight.

PROVERBS 3:5-6 NASB

Father, I know I can be completely honest with You because You know what word I'll say before it's even on my lips. So when I tell You that I struggle with trusting in myself, it comes as no surprise to You. The fact is that I do lean on my own understanding. I try to figure things out on my own. I try to set my own course and live my own way. But Lord, I need You. I need to trust You with all of my heart. I need to lean on Your understanding. I want to acknowledge You in all of my ways because You are the living God. It's a bonus that You'll make my paths straight and help make sense of my life. I believe this. Please help me stop trying to direct my own life and instead live out my belief in You. In Jesus' name I pray, amen.

WEIGHED DOWN

But You, O LORD, are a shield about me,
my glory, and the One who lifts my head.
I was crying to the LORD with my voice,
and He answered me from His holy mountain.
PSALM 3:3–4 NASB

Father, tonight I come to You weighed down by life. I cry out to You—literally crying about what's going on. You know the details. You know what burdens my heart. You know what I can't get off my mind. Even in all of my despair, frustration, and sadness, I pray I'll rest in the way. You're my shield of protection. You and You alone are my glory—my excellence! You lift my head as it's heavy with tears and exhaustion. I am so thankful I can come to You for comfort. I praise You for Your goodness and Your never-ending love for me. Thank You for listening to my prayers and answering them. I love You so very much. In Jesus' name I pray, amen.

WHAT SHOULD I WEAR?

"Why are you worried about clothing? Observe how the lilies of the field grow; they do not toil nor do they spin, yet I say to you that not even Solomon in all his glory clothed himself like one of these. But if God so clothes the grass of the field, which is alive today and tomorrow is thrown into the furnace, will He not much more clothe you?"

MATTHEW 6:28-30 NASB

Father, in Your Word, Jesus promised that I don't have to worry about the clothing I wear. That is so different than the focus of the world. But just like You clothe the lilies of the field so beautifully, You'll clothe me too. I pray You'll help me be content with what I wear and that I'll modestly protect my body. Please help me see the wonderful ways You actually do bring outfits and clothing into my life—ways that I don't have to worry about or consider. Thank You for faithfully and generously providing for all my needs and so many of my wants. You are so good to me! In Jesus' name I pray, amen.

CHOSEN BY YOU

*He predestined us to adoption as sons
through Jesus Christ to Himself, according
to the kind intention of His will, to the praise
of the glory of His grace, which He freely
bestowed on us in the Beloved.*

EPHESIANS 1:5–6 NASB

Father, I admit that I don't understand Your plans or Your choices. But even when I can't understand something, I can still appreciate it. So tonight I thank You for choosing to adopt me. You could choose absolutely anyone (and You do!), so to know that You've chosen me is amazing. You are so kind, and Your will reflects Your kindness. I praise You and Your grace, and I thank You for giving it to me so generously through Jesus. I don't deserve it, but even so, I pray I might start living my life in a way that is worthy of You and Your gift—and that I'll never take You for granted. In Jesus' name I pray, amen.

WATCH YOURSELF!

Brothers and sisters, if someone is caught in a sin, you who live by the Spirit should restore that person gently. But watch yourselves, or you also may be tempted.

GALATIANS 6:1 NIV

Father, I found out that one of my friends is sinning. The thing is, I don't know if my friend is even sorry. It almost seems like my friend is enjoying the sin. I'm upset by it—and I don't want to follow the same path. Could You please help me? I'd like to follow Your Word and try to gently help my friend get back to the right way. But I'm worried I'll be tempted in the process. Please keep me from temptation and from falling into the same sin. I love You and want to do what's right in Your eyes. In Jesus' name I pray, amen.

BULLIED

*But the salvation of the righteous is from
the LORD; He is their strength in time of trouble.
The LORD helps them and delivers them;
He delivers them from the wicked and saves
them, because they take refuge in Him.*

PSALM 37:39-40 NASB

Father God, I'm so glad You're for me because it feels like so many people are against me. The bullies in my life seem so wicked. They do and say such horrible things. My heart feels broken, and my confidence is shattered. Please help me remember that You don't see me the same way they do, and most people don't see me that way either. I pray You'll be my strength when it doesn't feel like I have any. Keep me safe from these bullies. I want to grow closer to You in this awful time—I run to You for help because I feel so helpless. I pray You'll bring something good out of these bad situations and help me shine Your light even when I don't feel like it. Instead of getting back at mean people, please help me treat them with love, just like Jesus did. In His name I pray, amen.

GOTTA HAVE FAITH

*Faith is confidence in what we hope for and
assurance about what we do not see.*
HEBREWS 11:1 NIV

Father God, I come to You tonight but admit that
sometimes I don't always know You're real. When You
seem so quiet, it's hard to remember that You're the
living God. I want to believe in You. I want to worship
the one true God. Please help me keep my faith in
You. Even when I don't feel like You're there, please
help me remember that faith is not a feeling, and the
truth of Your existence doesn't depend on whether
I can see or feel or hear You. You are there. You are
real, living, and You are at work in the world today.
Thank You for loving me even when I'm tempted to
doubt You. In Jesus' name I pray, amen.

SEEK PEACE AND PURSUE IT

Whoever of you loves life and desires to see many good days, keep your tongue from evil and your lips from telling lies. Turn from evil and do good; seek peace and pursue it.

PSALM 34:12–14 NIV

Heavenly Father, sometimes it's so tough to live in peace with other people. But even when I see conflict all around me, I want to choose peace. I want to do good. I want to let Your peace shine through my life. When people are stressed and worried, please help me be a peaceful influence. In the heat of the moment, help me to remember that my mouth has a lot to do with keeping peace. I know the words I choose have influence and power. I pray You'll use me and my words to calm people down in a gentle, kind way. Where there's trouble, I don't want to add to the conflict by what I say or do. Please use me as a peacemaker. In Jesus' name I pray, amen.

Different Than the World

But Noah found favor in the eyes of
the Lord. . . . And Noah did all that
the Lord had commanded him.

GENESIS 6:8; 7:5 ESV

Lord God, You have such a wonderful way of not only knowing Your children but also caring for them. You've proven this time and again in my life and in Your Word through stories like Noah's. Even though Noah lived in a wicked, wicked world, he still honored and obeyed You. In fact, he did everything You commanded him, no matter what others around him said or did. And when he followed You, he found favor in Your eyes. Just like Noah, many days it feels like I'm living in a wicked world. I pray that even if my obedience to You makes me completely different than everyone else around me, I'll obey anyway. I want to follow You and do all that You command me to do. I want to trust You and You alone. It's my heart's true desire to find favor in Your eyes. I love You and want to honor You every day of my life. In Jesus' name I pray, amen.

A LIVING HOPE

Praise be to the God and Father of our Lord Jesus Christ! In his great mercy he has given us new birth into a living hope through the resurrection of Jesus Christ from the dead, and into an inheritance that can never perish, spoil or fade. This inheritance is kept in heaven for you, who through faith are shielded by God's power until the coming of the salvation that is ready to be revealed in the last time.

1 PETER 1:3–5 NIV

God and Father, thank You for Your mercy that I don't deserve. And thank You for hope that is real and living. As I hope in You, I wait in certainty for what I know will come. I look forward to what's waiting for me in heaven. It won't ever fade or spoil! Even though it may seem like a very long time until that's my reality, I can start looking forward to it. I'm thankful that in my everyday life, You shield me with Your power and guarantee my future. I praise You for the way You care for me today and will continue to care for me forever. In Jesus' name I pray, amen.

GUARD YOUR HEART!

*Above all else, guard your heart,
for everything you do flows from it.*
PROVERBS 4:23 NIV

Lord God, I know my heart is an important part of me that guides my thoughts and decisions. So often, this culture tells me to follow my heart. But sometimes I'm not exactly sure what I'm following. My feelings seem to go all over the place—every day they seem to change, and even moment by moment. Some days it feels like I'm on a wild roller-coaster ride. Instead of trusting my ever-changing feelings, I pray that I'll start to guard my heart more carefully. Please help me keep bad influences out and cling to the good influences that please You. Give me wisdom, Father, to know what needs to stay in my heart—and what things need to go. In Jesus' name I pray, amen.

GET WELL SOON

Have mercy on me, LORD, for I am faint;
heal me, LORD, for my bones are in agony.
PSALM 6:2 NIV

Father, I haven't been feeling very good lately. And I'm tempted to let that affect my moods and attitudes. I know all things happen for a reason, but, Father, I wish I didn't have to feel this way! I pray You'll heal me. Please restore my health and help me feel better. When I'm tempted to worry about what's wrong, please fill me with peace. When I want to complain about how I feel, please help me keep a good attitude. And I pray I could get plenty of rest and feel like myself again. In Jesus' name I pray, amen.

BECOMING A DO-GOODER

*And let us not grow weary of doing good, for in
due season we will reap, if we do not give up.*
GALATIANS 6:9 ESV

Father God, sometimes it feels like I try so hard to
do good—to make life better for other people, to
do my best, to be a good example of what it's like
to follow You. But all of that goodness wears me
out. I get tired. I pray that even if I'm feeling weary,
You'll give me the strength to keep on keeping on. I
don't want to be a quitter. And I really don't want to
give up and stop doing good things. Please help me
see even just a tiny result of what my good works
are accomplishing for You in the people around me.
I love You and I want to serve You with my life. In
Jesus' name I pray, amen.

NOT MY OWN

*Do you not know that your bodies are temples of the
Holy Spirit, who is in you, whom you have received
from God? You are not your own; you were bought
at a price. Therefore honor God with your bodies.*

1 CORINTHIANS 6:19–20 NIV

Father God, in today's world, it is so hard to honor
You with my body. Impurity is everywhere. From things
people say to things people do—both in person and
on social media—purity has become something so
foreign. Yet as strange as purity seems today, truth
hasn't changed. My body is a temple of the Holy
Spirit. Your Spirit is living inside of me; You've given
Him to me as proof that I'm Yours. And as a temple
of Your Holy Spirit, I need to live like it. I'm not my
own! As much as I might be tempted to do whatever
I'd like with my body, it's not mine to mistreat. I need
to honor You with my body, even if it's unpopular or
if I feel like I'd rather do something else. Please help
me remember I was bought at a huge price, and help
me honor Christ's sacrifice with my purity. In Jesus'
name I pray, amen.

WALKING THE WALK

*Therefore as you have received Christ Jesus
the Lord, so walk in Him, having been firmly
rooted and now being built up in Him and
established in your faith, just as you were
instructed, and overflowing with gratitude.*
COLOSSIANS 2:6–7 NASB

Father, thank You for Jesus. And thank You for His
love for me. I believe He is Your Son who led a perfect life then died a cruel death on the cross. And I
believe His death paid for my sins. Because I believe
He is the only way, the only truth, and the only life,
I boldly come to You through Him. I receive Christ
Jesus as my Lord. I trust He has forgiven me of my
sins. I pray that with this new life and forgiveness, I
would be rooted and built up in Him. May the things
I think, say, and do every day be filled with faith and
devotion to You. In Jesus' name I pray, amen.

Together

Only let your manner of life be worthy of the gospel of Christ, so that whether I come and see you or am absent, I may hear of you that you are standing firm in one spirit, with one mind striving side by side for the faith of the gospel, and not frightened in anything by your opponents. This is a clear sign to them of their destruction, but of your salvation, and that from God.

PHILIPPIANS 1:27–28 ESV

Lord Jesus, I want my life to be worthy of You. And I pray that my life will be joined to the lives of other believers. If I'm not letting believers into my life right now, please bless me with good relationships—mentors and friends who can help keep me close to You and who love You. I pray that through fellowship, we can encourage one another to stand firm and strive for the faith of the Gospel. Please help us cheer one another on and not be scared of things in this world. Thank You that I don't have to face this Christian walk all on my own. In Your name I pray, amen.

WHAT IS TRUTH?

*Jesus answered, "You say correctly that I am
a king. For this I have been born, and for this I
have come into the world, to testify to the truth.
Everyone who is of the truth hears My voice."
Pilate said to Him, "What is truth?"*

JOHN 18:37–38 NASB

Lord, so much is confusing in today's world. And there's so much noise with people sharing their ideas of what's right and wrong. When I listen to what everybody says, I hear many contradicting opinions, and nothing seems to make sense. I pray that I will know and understand Your truth and let it guide my life. In fact, please help it transform the decisions I make and the way I think and live. Thank You that Your Word is true. Thank You that Jesus alone is the way, the truth, and the life. In His name I pray, amen.

TRUST

Trust in the LORD and do good; dwell in the land and cultivate faithfulness. Delight yourself in the LORD; and He will give you the desires of your heart.

PSALM 37:3–4 NASB

Father God, the thought of delighting myself in You is special. I can completely enjoy You—enjoy being with You and enjoy getting to know You better. As I delight in You more and more, I naturally trust You more and more. And trusting in You adds so much peace to my life. I don't have to worry about what could happen; I get to rest in the fact that You are God. And as I trust in You and delight myself in You, great things happen: I end up doing good, I'm faithful to You, and a huge bonus is that You'll give me the desires of my heart. I pray You'll shape the desires of my heart as You give them to me faithfully. Thank You that I can trust You, Father! In Jesus' name I pray, amen.

AFRAID AND DISCOURAGED? OR STRONG AND COURAGEOUS?

"Have I not commanded you? Be strong and courageous. Do not be afraid; do not be discouraged, for the LORD your God will be with you wherever you go."

JOSHUA 1:9 NIV

Father, I'm so thankful I can trust You. And I'm so thankful You're in control. Because, Lord, I'm scared. I don't want to do what I have to do. I don't feel like being brave. In fact, I'm so nervous I feel like I just want to hide. But I know I need to be brave. I need a bunch of courage to face what I don't want to face. And I need to remember what's true: You're with me wherever I go. I don't have to be afraid or discouraged. Through You, I can be strong and courageous. I want to trust You. Please help me find my courage and strength in You. In Jesus' name I pray, amen.

PERFECT LOVE

The LORD will keep you from all harm—he will watch over your life; the LORD will watch over your coming and going both now and forevermore.

PSALM 121:7–8 NIV

Father, it's such a comfort to know You'll keep me from all harm. Tonight, I can go to sleep in peace knowing that You watch over my life—now and forever. You love me with a perfect love that is beyond my understanding. But knowing that You watch over me and protect me is just part of the proof of Your love. I pray that when I'm feeling anxious, You'll remind me of Your love and protection. Please help me walk confidently through each day, knowing that You are with me and for me. Rather than being overcome by fear, I can experience the peace of Your love and confidence that nothing in this world can take away. Thank You for this great gift. In Jesus' name I pray, amen.

LEARNiNG TO TAKE ADViCE

*"Hear instruction and be wise,
and do not neglect it."*

PROVERBS 8:33 ESV

Father, I admit that sometimes (okay—most times) I want to have my own way. I know what I want to do—and then I want to do it. I also think I know what's best for me. It's hard for me to realize that I don't always know what's best. And it's really hard to accept the fact that other people can help point me in the right direction. Even if I don't always want to listen to advice from my parents or teachers, please help me remember they've lived through teenage years before. If they have my best interests at heart, please help me to not shut out their instruction but instead to listen to them and then make a wise decision. It might mean that I totally listen to them, trust my own judgment, or combine the two. Whatever I choose, though, let it glorify You. In Jesus' name I pray, amen.

WHAT AM I?

When I look at your heavens, the work of your
fingers, the moon and the stars, which you have set
in place, what is man that you are mindful of him,
and the son of man that you care for him?
PSALM 8:3-4 ESV

Creator God, I am in awe of You. You've created
everything—everything! When I look around and see
the sunrise and sunset, it's obvious that You are the ultimate artist. When I see the moon and stars at night
and think about how little I am and how humongous
the universe is, I'm amazed. It's mind-boggling to think
of the way You've created humans so intricately and
so uniquely. There are many people in this world—and
You know the hearts and minds of every single one.
No one escapes Your notice. What are we, that You
would do that? What have I ever done to deserve
Your love and mercy? Every day You care for me so
wonderfully. I may not fully appreciate each day, but
You still care for me and provide for me. My heart is
beating and there's breath in my lungs. Thank You!
In Jesus' name I pray, amen.

FRiENDS FOREVER

The friendship of the LORD is for those who fear
him, and he makes known to them his covenant.

PSALM 25:14 ESV

Lord, sometimes I feel so lonely. It doesn't seem like I have any true friends. It's been easy for me to fall into a trap of trusting in my friends and basing my happiness on them. When I feel loved and included, life is great. And I'm sent crashing down whenever I feel snubbed and intentionally left out. The amazing thing is, though, that You are my friend. You're my best friend. You let me know Your covenant and have promised incredible things—and I'm grateful. Even though I don't always feel like I can measure up to You as the kind of friend You deserve, I'm in awe of You. And in that awe, I fear Your power as well. I recognize who You are and am amazed You'd reach out to me in friendship. Thank You for Your love and kindness! You are the best friend of all. In Jesus' name I pray, amen.

YOUR LITTLE LAMB

*"I am the good shepherd; I know my sheep
and my sheep know me—just as the Father
knows me and I know the Father—and I
lay down my life for the sheep."*

JOHN 10:14–15 NIV

Lord Jesus, when I think of sheep, I picture cute little fluffy animals. But even though they are adorable, sheep are pretty dumb. They love to wander and get themselves into trouble. Sheep need someone to lead them and guide them—to keep them safe and out of danger. And they know their shepherd's voice and listen only to him. Just like those sweet but naive sheep, I need You to lead me and guide me. Please keep me safe and out of danger. I pray I'll know You and Your voice and listen to You. I'm Your little lamb. Thank You for caring for me and coming to give me life. Because of You, I don't lack a single thing. You calm me down and gently show me the way I should go. You're a very good Shepherd. In Your name I pray, amen.

MORE AND MORE

*As for other matters, brothers and sisters, we
instructed you how to live in order to please God,
as in fact you are living. Now we ask you and urge
you in the Lord Jesus to do this more and more.*

1 THESSALONIANS 4:1 NIV

Lord Jesus, it's so tempting to live for myself every
day. Looking for pleasure or trying to live for the
moment seems really appealing. Yet what I need to
do—and what's so much better to do—is to live in a
way that will please You. Deep down, I want to please
You. And I know the difference between right and
wrong, good choices and bad choices. Just because
I know what I should do, though, doesn't mean that
it's easy to choose to do what pleases You. I pray
You'll speak to my conscience when I'm tempted
to sin and wander from Your purpose and plan for
me. I pray I'll please and obey You more and more,
until the desires of this world fade away. In Your
name I pray, amen.

UNWORTHY...BUT GRATEFUL

*In him we have redemption through his blood,
the forgiveness of sins, in accordance with the
riches of God's grace that he lavished on us.*

 EPHESIANS 1:7–8 NIV

Jesus, You are perfect, and I am so not perfect. But You chose to love me anyway. And You do so much more than love me! You gave Your very life for me so I could be brought into a relationship with You. You bought me at a price. And You've forgiven me of my sins. I have a lot of them, and You know every single one, yet You still forgive me. As if that wasn't enough, You lavish me with undeserved riches. I'm unworthy but thankful. In Your name I pray, amen.

WHITE AS SNOW

"Come now, let us settle the matter," says the
LORD. "Though your sins are like scarlet, they
shall be as white as snow; though they are
red as crimson, they shall be like wool."

ISAIAH 1:18 NIV

Lord Jesus, I thank You that the Bible is filled with such vivid word pictures. My sins are like scarlet. I'm guilty, and it's like my sin has stained and given me a bright red color. But You've taken that away. Your forgiveness washes me and turns me into a brand-new creation. Through Your sacrifice for me, I'm clean. In Your eyes, my crimson stain is gone, and now I'm white as snow. You've saved me. You've forgiven my sins. And my guilt and shame are gone. I can never thank You enough for Your amazing gift. You are so good to me! In Your name I pray, amen.

MY HEART AT PEACE

A heart at peace gives life to the body,
but envy rots the bones.
PROVERBS 14:30 NIV

Father God, I long for peace. I know You give peace—in fact, it comes naturally when I'm living in step with Your Holy Spirit. But sometimes I just don't feel at peace. When my heart is calm and resting in You, I feel more alive. I'm happy and content with what I have. And when I'm not at peace? Ew. So often, jealousy and envy rob my peace and take my eyes off all You've given me. I look and see what other people have and wonder why it can't be mine. The truth is, though, You've given me what's best for me. And You know so much better than I do. Please help me learn how to be content in any circumstance so I can experience Your true peace. In Jesus' name I pray, amen.

SUCH A TIME AS THIS

*"And who knows whether you have not come
to the kingdom for such a time as this?"*
ESTHER 4:14 ESV

Father, You have blessed me with so much, and I don't want to take it for granted. Yet so often, I feel like time is going really slowly. I know I should appreciate where I am right now. Amazingly, You've chosen this exact time and place in history for me. You know this is when and where I should be. Please help me keep that in mind when I'd rather speed up time. Sometimes—many times—I'd rather fast-forward. What will I be like as a woman? What will I do? Will I get married or have children? Where will I live? I have so many questions, and I'd love to know the answers. But for now, I need to wait for You and Your timing. In my waiting, please help me enjoy all of Your daily gifts. In Jesus' name I pray, amen.

UNCHANGING

Every good and perfect gift is from above,
coming down from the Father of the heavenly
lights, who does not change like shifting shadows.
JAMES 1:17 NIV

Father, it's amazing that You never change. You are
who You say You are. You are my rock, my firm foundation. Everything in this world feels like it shifts and
changes. But You stay the same. You never move, and
You never leave me. Thank You for being constant.
Thank You for being the One I can completely trust.
You know just what I need and when I need it—and
You generously give to me. Every single good and
perfect gift comes from You. Thank You for being so
good to me! I love You. In Jesus' name I pray, amen.

MAKING LIFE BETTER

*The memory of the righteous is a blessing,
but the name of the wicked will rot.*

PROVERBS 10:7 ESV

Father God, sometimes it's hard to keep in mind that the little things I say or do leave an impression on other people. In fact, how I treat people now will change the way they'll always remember me. I want people to smile when they think of me—I want memories of me to be good. I definitely don't want others to think negatively whenever I come to mind. Even for people who aren't my family or close friends, please help me to bless their lives just by being myself. I pray that tomorrow You'll use me to make someone's day better. Please help me be an encouragement and let my life reflect Your love. I love You and know it is a huge honor to be able to represent You right where I am. In Jesus' name I pray, amen.

FOLLOWING HIS LEAD

I will praise the LORD, who counsels me;
even at night my heart instructs me. I keep
my eyes always on the LORD. With him at
my right hand, I will not be shaken.

PSALM 16:7–8 NIV

Lord, I praise You! You are so good to me, especially in the way You lovingly and gently guide me. I trust that You'll continue to lead and instruct me even while I sleep. Please help me listen to You and follow. I pray I'll keep my eyes on You and not look to my own ways. It's hard to not chase after the things I think I want. Instead, I trust You'll help me choose what's right in Your eyes. I'd love my days to feel steady and sure, and if I follow You closely, I know I won't be shaken. Thank You for counseling me—I pray I'll gladly welcome it, even when what You ask me to do is different than what I'd choose. I want to follow Your lead. In Jesus' name I pray, amen.

TO HAVE A FRiEND
IS TO BE A FRiEND

One who has unreliable friends soon
comes to ruin, but there is a friend
who sticks closer than a brother.

PROVERBS 18:24 NIV

Lord God, Your Word says that Jesus is a friend who sticks closer than a brother and that a friend loves at all times. That means it's important for me to be a good friend not just when times are fun. To be a good friend, I need to stick with my friend in hard times, through challenges, and through heartbreaking moments. Please help me be the kind of friend I would like to have, even when it's uncomfortable. Please help me be dependable and caring. Please help me look for and find ways to make my friends' days better. Please help me encourage and love my friends well out of the abundant love You've given me. In Jesus' name I pray, amen.

CHOOSE YOUR WORDS

"Whoever would love life and see good
days must keep their tongue from evil
and their lips from deceitful speech."

1 PETER 3:10 NIV

Lord Jesus, I would love to see good days. And the thought of loving my life—instead of just enduring or even hating it—is really fantastic. I would like to enjoy and appreciate my life and to have a life worth enjoying and appreciating. But I often forget that my mouth and my words have the power to change everything. Please help me learn right now as a teenager that what I choose to say—or not say—makes a huge difference. And please help me keep my tongue from evil and my lips from deceiving others. I don't want to be two-faced. I don't want to say things that hurt others or bring shame to You, Lord. Please help me to choose my words wisely so that I may have a good life! In Your name I pray, amen.

FOCUS

*Since, then, you have been raised with Christ,
set your hearts on things above, where Christ is,
seated at the right hand of God.*

COLOSSIANS 3:1 NIV

Father, thank You for Jesus! Thank You for His perfect life—and His complete sacrifice that paid for my sins. It's easy to focus on myself and the things of this world, but I pray You might help me seek things that are above. Please take my focus off of myself. I don't want to selfishly think about me, me, me all the time. Instead, set my mind and the direction of my life on You and Your good works. Please help me live a life of love and faith in You. I pray I wouldn't get bogged down with what other people think is so important—grades, clothes, belongings, relationships, or popularity. Help me focus on You and You alone. In Jesus' name I pray, amen.

TRUSTWORTHY

Blessed is the man who makes the LORD
his trust, who does not turn to the proud,
to those who go astray after a lie!

PSALM 40:4 ESV

Father, I'm so glad You're worthy of my trust. I'm so thankful You are my God. And I'm grateful I can put my trust in You and You alone. I don't want to turn away from You. This world is filled with so many people and things that are fighting for my attention and affection. I don't want my heart to follow a lie. I don't want to give my time and thoughts to anything that would lead me astray from You. Please help me realize what the things of this world are—and help me turn away from them. I want to keep my eyes on You and trust You completely. In Jesus' name I pray, amen.

MY REASON FOR HOPE

Let us hold unswervingly to the hope we
profess, for he who promised is faithful.
HEBREWS 10:23 NIV

Father God, I put my faith in You completely and totally. I believe You are who You say You are. I believe Jesus is Your perfect Son who came to pay for my sins with His life. I trust You and I expect all that You've promised will come true in Your perfect timing. Time and time again You've proven Yourself to be constant in my life. It's wonderful that, in hope, I can look forward to what You'll do next. I may not know what each day will bring, but I know that You are faithful. And You're in the middle of weaving together something very beautiful in and through my life. Even if things look or feel messy right now, You can and will make something absolutely beautiful from my mess. Thank You! In Jesus' name I pray, amen.

PUTTING OTHERS FIRST

Do nothing out of selfish ambition or vain conceit.
Rather, in humility value others above yourselves,
not looking to your own interests but each of
you to the interests of the others.

PHILIPPIANS 2:3–4 NIV

Father, just like the old saying goes, "It's hard to be humble." Pride has such a sneaky way of creeping into my thoughts and beliefs. I think I'm better than I really am. I feel like I deserve so much. But I want to try to live like Jesus did—and He was totally humble. He gave up everything to come to earth as a man, and not even a king with life in a luxurious palace and a bunch of servants. No, he came to serve others. I pray I'd be more like Him and stop focusing on my own interests or what's best for me. Instead, please help me look to what other people need. Help me figure out how I can best help them without thinking of what could be in it for me. In Jesus' name I pray, amen.

ANGER ISSUES

Be not quick in your spirit to become angry,
for anger lodges in the heart of fools.

ECCLESIASTES 7:9 ESV

Heavenly Father, sometimes I get so angry—or at least I feel anger brewing inside me. I know I shouldn't be this way. And really, I don't like getting angry because I know it affects every part of me. It feels like it gets lodged in my heart and changes the way I think and speak and respond to others—and to You. When I'm tempted to let anger build up and simmer, could You please extinguish it? Please help me remember that this life is too short to waste my time getting angry. Instead, please help me find a better way to deal with my frustration, let it go, and move on. And, as hard as it may seem, please help me forgive others like You've forgiven me. Thank You for filling me with Your Holy Spirit, who can help me get past my anger issues. In Jesus' name I pray, amen.

I LOVE you!

*Though you have not seen him, you love him.
Though you do not now see him, you believe in
him and rejoice with joy that is inexpressible
and filled with glory, obtaining the outcome
of your faith, the salvation of your souls.*

1 PETER 1:8–9 ESV

Jesus, faith is a pretty exciting thing. Even though I've never seen You, I have complete faith in You. I know You're real. I know You're alive. And I love You. I do believe in You. And in my belief and faith, You fill me with joy I can't explain. Sometimes it feels like I might explode with joy! I pray I'll live out my faith in You—that my joy and peace will be contagious and that I'll be able to love people really, really well. Thank You for saving me and filling me with such wonderful feelings. In Your name I pray, amen.

BEAUTY...AND THE BEAST?

*Like a gold ring in a pig's snout is a
beautiful woman without discretion.*

PROVERBS 11:22 ESV

Father, I admit that I focus on my looks a lot. Sometimes I wish my face or body or hair was different. Other times I spend too much time thinking about the clothes or shoes I wear. I think about how much I weigh and how tall I am. And for some reason, I wonder what I should change or how I could change my appearance. In my own way, I try to figure out how to make myself look more desirable—either to other people or myself. Father, I pray that I'll become content with the way You've created me. I pray that my true beauty would be found in my heart, and that I would be wise too. Please help me not just focus on my looks but on wisdom and judgment, so I don't end up like a gold ring in a pig's snout! I pray my life will be precious and valuable, and not a foolish waste. In Jesus' name I pray, amen.

STEP BY STEP

My steps have held fast to Your paths.
My feet have not slipped.
PSALM 17:5 NASB

Father God, knowing that You'll direct each of my steps is a huge comfort. I pray that I'll willingly stay to Your paths, not wandering outside of Your will. As You guide me, You won't let my feet slip. I don't have to worry about stumbling and falling when I'm walking through life with You. Even if I don't know where I'm going in the future—I don't even know where Your path will lead me tomorrow!—I pray I'll confidently walk the path You have me on right now. I absolutely trust that You know where You're taking me, and You'll stay with me when the road seems rough. Thank You for lovingly guiding me and for having a plan for my life. In Jesus' name I pray, amen.

CHOOSING MY FRIENDS

Blessed is the one who does not walk in step with the wicked or stand in the way that sinners take or sit in the company of mockers, but whose delight is in the law of the LORD, and who meditates on his law day and night.

PSALM 1:1–2 NIV

Lord, I pray You'll give me wisdom when it comes to choosing my friends. I really don't want to spend time with the wicked because I don't want their habits to rub off on me. Your Word tells me that bad company corrupts good character, and that means I'm affected and changed by my friends. Because of that, I want to make wise choices when it comes to relationships. Please surround me with friends who love You. I pray my friends and I could help one another grow closer to You. Please help us to know Your Word better and better and encourage one another to live out Your truth in what we say and do. I'm excited to see the friends You'll bring into my life! In Jesus' name I pray, amen.

ASHAMED?

"If anyone is ashamed of me and my words in this adulterous and sinful generation, the Son of Man will be ashamed of them when he comes in his Father's glory with the holy angels."

MARK 8:38 NIV

Lord Jesus, I hate to admit this to You, but You know all—and I feel like I need to confess. Sometimes I'm afraid to stand up for You. When people say awful things or use Your name in vain, I'm quiet. Instead of speaking up for what is right, I don't. Could You please help me be bolder for You, Lord? I'm not ashamed of You and Your words. At least I don't want to be. Could You please help me stand up for Your truth? And stand up for You? I want to be a good example and witness for You in this world. I love You. In Jesus' name I pray, amen.

SETTING AN EXAMPLE

Don't let anyone look down on you because you are young, but set an example for the believers in speech, in conduct, in love, in faith and in purity.

1 TIMOTHY 4:12 NIV

Father God, in the big scope of things, I know I'm insignificant—just a teensy blip in the picture of eternity. Even if this is true, I still hope You'll use me to make a difference in the world today. Please help me make my family better just by being a part of it. Please help me step out in boldness and faith and make my school a better place. Even if it takes a lot of effort and not focusing on myself so much, please help me make life better for people who meet me. In other words, please make my life count. Make my existence matter. And help me improve the lives of everyone who knows me. In Jesus' name I pray, amen.

GUARANTEED

In him you also, when you heard the word of truth,
the gospel of your salvation, and believed in him,
were sealed with the promised Holy Spirit, who is
the guarantee of our inheritance until we acquire
possession of it, to the praise of his glory.

EPHESIANS 1:13–14 ESV

Lord, I thank You for Your Holy Spirit. I thank You for what a gift He is to believers like me. It might be awhile until I see You in heaven, but until then, Your Spirit is proof that I'm Yours. I've been saved through believing in Jesus. And I've been sealed, or protected, through Your Holy Spirit. All of this amazingness is to Your praise! And all of this brings You glory. Thank You for Your plan and providing something I could never do on my own. Thank You for Jesus. And thank You for the way Your Spirit guarantees my future with You. In Jesus' name I pray, amen.

COME WITH CONFIDENCE

Let us then approach God's throne of grace with confidence, so that we may receive mercy and find grace to help us in our time of need.

HEBREWS 4:16 NIV

Father, so often I feel like I need to come to You with my act all together. But because I feel like a hot mess and like I'm so far from perfect, sometimes I feel like I shouldn't come to You. Yet You've promised that I can approach You with confidence. You have a throne of grace—undeserved favor! And when I come near to You, You lavish me with Your mercy and grace. You help me when I need it the most. I need You and Your forgiveness and comfort. I draw near to You tonight, Abba Father. I pray You'll bless me with joy and peace as I rest and hope in You. I love You. In Jesus' name I pray, amen.

WHY WORRY?

"Therefore do not worry about tomorrow,
for tomorrow will worry about itself.
Each day has enough trouble of its own."
MATTHEW 6:34 NIV

Father God, I believe in Your Word. I believe it's true. And I desperately need to remember and choose to believe its truth tonight. Lord, I'm nervous about tomorrow. I know Your Word tells me I don't have to worry about tomorrow. But I'm really tempted to obsess and get anxious about things. When I'm stressed, please replace those feelings with peace. When I'm dwelling on everything that could or might happen, please help me stick to the facts and not live in what-ifs. And when I start physically feeling the effects of my anxiety, please help me take a deep breath and relax. Thank You that I can trust in You completely. In Jesus' name I pray, amen.

PREVENTING A CALLOUS

He said, "Go and tell this people: 'Be ever hearing, but never understanding; be ever seeing, but never perceiving.' Make the heart of this people calloused; make their ears dull and close their eyes. Otherwise they might see with their eyes, hear with their ears, understand with their hearts, and turn and be healed."

ISAIAH 6:9–10 NIV

Father, I know You can make hearts calloused, just like You can make ears dull or close eyes. I pray this wouldn't happen in my life though! Please help me realize that every time I turn from You and Your commands, I get a callous. And eventually, all of those calluses build up and I just won't hear or see You at work. I want to hear and understand You. I want to see and recognize You. Please keep my heart tender to You and Your leading. Shape me into the girl You would like me to become—a girl who's quick to listen and obey. I want to see with my eyes, hear with my ears, understand with my heart, and turn and be healed. In Jesus' name I pray, amen.

NO, NOT ONE

"None is righteous, no, not one; no one understands; no one seeks for God. All have turned aside; together they have become worthless; no one does good, not even one."

ROMANS 3:10–12 ESV

Father God, why do people turn away from You? Why don't people seek You? How I wish I wouldn't be like everyone else! On my own, I'm imperfect; I realize that every single day. I try to not sin, but perfection and righteousness are things I could never accomplish on my own. Perfection is through Christ alone, and it's to Him I turn. I don't want to turn aside. I don't want to be worthless. Through Jesus, please help me to do good here on earth. While I have breath in my lungs, please count me righteous through Christ alone. In Jesus' name I pray, amen.

SCHOOL STRUGGLES

A sluggard's appetite is never filled, but the
desires of the diligent are fully satisfied.
PROVERBS 13:4 NIV

Father, I'm glad I can come to You at any time with anything. Lately I've felt pretty frustrated with a particular subject at school. As much as I want to succeed, something's just not right. I don't know what to change or how exactly to improve. But I ask You to please help me. Please help things make sense. Help me to find the strength and determination to work as hard as I can. I want to work for You—and You alone. Please help me forget about the pressure to succeed. I pray that even when this class feels so difficult and confusing, You'll help me focus on working hard to glorify You. In Jesus' name I pray, amen.

KEEP YOUR WAY PURE

How can a young person stay on the path
of purity? By living according to your word.
I seek you with all my heart; do not let
me stray from your commands.

PSALM 119:9–10 NIV

Father, in today's world it's so hard to know what is right—and then choose to do it. Please help me to know what would please You. Help me seek it out in Your Word then live by it. And please keep my feet on the path of purity. I do seek You with all of my heart, and I do want to follow Your commands. Thank You that they'll help me make the right choices and live the right way. There is a right way and a wrong way to live. And there is a path of purity and a path of impurity. Please help me stay on the right, pure path so I can live a life that makes You happy and be a good example of what a Christ follower is like. In Jesus' name I pray, amen.

PAYBACK?

Make sure that nobody pays back wrong
for wrong, but always strive to do what is
good for each other and for everyone else.

1 Thessalonians 5:15 NIV

Lord Jesus, living for You can seem so difficult at times. Sometimes I feel selfish and want to do what's right for me. And when people treat me poorly, so often my first thought is figuring out a way I could get back at them. But I'm Your child! And You live in me. Because of that, I don't have to pay back wrong for any wrong done to me. I can choose to forgive other people and treat them with kindness. I pray I'll seek to do what is good for other people. Please help me unselfishly look past my own agenda and interests. Please help me look past myself and find ways to help other people out of love for You. Please help me be a good example for You. In Your name I pray, amen.

NO REGRETS

For the sorrow that is according to
the will of God produces a repentance
without regret, leading to salvation,
but the sorrow of the world produces death.

2 Corinthians 7:10 nasb

Father God, it's so easy to live with regrets. Choices I make seem wrong. Sometimes I can't believe the things I say or do. Can You please help me? I'd love to make choices that honor You. Those choices will help me live a life without regrets. In the heat of the moment, please give me enough wisdom to choose something that pleases You and will make my future self satisfied. I pray that I'll be able to live tomorrow without regrets. If and when I do make a bad choice, please help me to quickly realize it and repent—not continue in my sin and add to my trouble. Please guide me. I want to follow You! In Jesus' name I pray, amen.

CHOSEN

Therefore, as God's chosen people, holy and dearly loved, clothe yourselves with compassion, kindness, humility, gentleness and patience.

COLOSSIANS 3:12 NIV

Father, You've chosen me! Every time I'm tempted to listen to voices that tell me I'm not wanted, accepted, or good enough, please remind me that You, the holy God of the universe, chose me. Help me to live like I've been chosen by You. Help me see the people throughout my day that need compassion—and then please give me strength and courage to reach out in love and understanding. Please help me be kind. I admit there are plenty of people in this world I'd rather not be kind to, but I know that kindness is possible through Your Holy Spirit. Please guard my life against pride and thinking of myself better than I should. Instead, please help me treat others as You'd like. In Jesus' name I pray, amen.

TRUST AND OBEY

Therefore, my dear friends, as you have always obeyed—not only in my presence, but now much more in my absence—continue to work out your salvation with fear and trembling, for it is God who works in you to will and to act in order to fulfill his good purpose.

PHILIPPIANS 2:12–13 NIV

Father God, I want to obey You. When sometimes I feel like I want to do my own thing and live life my own way, please help me remember that You'll direct my paths. That is such a comfort and a gift! Out of so much honor and respect for You, the Lord of the universe, I trust that You'll keep working in my life. Please fulfill Your good purpose for me. I'm humbled that You have a good purpose for me and that You'll act to make it happen. Thanks for choosing to use me. In Jesus' name I pray, amen.

NOTHING

For I am convinced that neither death nor life, neither angels nor demons, neither the present nor the future, nor any powers, neither height nor depth, nor anything else in all creation, will be able to separate us from the love of God that is in Christ Jesus our Lord.

ROMANS 8:38–39 NIV

Lord Jesus, the fact that absolutely nothing can or will separate me from the love of God that is in You is so amazing. Nothing will separate me from the love found in You. Nothing in this life. Not even death. Nothing I did in my past or am doing right now. Nothing I'll do in the future. Not angels or demons or anything else that's ever been or will be created. I'm completely safe and secure in Your love. This fact alone will help me sleep sweetly, resting in You tonight. I love You. In Jesus' name I pray, amen.

WHO'S IN CONTROL?

Trust in him at all times, O people; pour out your heart before him; God is a refuge for us.

PSALM 62:8 ESV

Father, tonight I need to remember that You're in control. I'm so glad You are because I feel like everything has spun out of my control. Control is such an illusion. Please help me rest in the fact that You know much more than I do about what is going on—and You know what I actually need and what is for my good. Deep down, I'm scared to let go of my hopes and dreams and place them in Your hands. But I know that I need to, and I want to release them to You. Please fill me with Your peace as I trust You with my life. In Jesus' name I pray, amen.

DOING A U-TURN

"Repent! Turn away from all your offenses;
then sin will not be your downfall."
EZEKIEL 18:30 NIV

Father, I have sinned against You. Today I gave into temptation, and I'm feeling so ashamed and unworthy. Please forgive me. I want to repent—not just ask for forgiveness but truly change and turn from that sin. Like a car doing a U-turn, I want to go in the other direction toward right choices that honor You. When Satan reminds me of my mistakes, please help me remember Your forgiveness. Jesus died for me; He was a perfect sacrifice for all my sins, just like my sins today. I don't deserve what He did for me, but I'm still thankful. Thank You, Lord, for forgiveness that I don't deserve and favor I never could earn. In Jesus' name I pray, amen.

PREPARED FOR ACTION

Therefore, prepare your minds for action,
keep sober in spirit, fix your hope completely
on the grace to be brought to you at the
revelation of Jesus Christ.

1 PETER 1:13 NASB

Lord Jesus, this world isn't an easy place to live in. You know that—that's why You came to save me. As I drift off to sleep and wake up to start a new day tomorrow, I pray You'll prepare my mind for action. Please help me remember that I can't just drift through life; I need to be serious about it. I need to protect my heart. I need to put my mind in gear. I want and need to fix all my hope on You and Your grace. When I'm tempted to go my own way, please reel me back in. Instead of floating along and taking whatever comes my way, please remind me that I need to actively live and make decisions that point to You and Your goodness in my life. In Your name I pray, amen.

RESTORE WHAT'S BROKEN

When the LORD takes pleasure in anyone's way,
he causes their enemies to make peace with them.

PROVERBS 16:7 NIV

Father God, thank You for Your gift of peace. Thank You that Your peace brings completeness and calm. I'm amazed and grateful that You have the power to restore what's broken and out of sorts—even relationships. At times it feels like it's impossible for me to make peace with someone when our relationship has been broken—or maybe our relationship never felt whole in the first place. But You make things right. You even cause my enemies to make peace with me. Please continue to mend what's broken in my life, especially when it comes to how I relate to others. With my whole heart, I pray that You would take pleasure in my way. May the things I say and do honor and please You. In Jesus' name I pray, amen.

WORDS AND MEDITATIONS

Let the words of my mouth and the meditation
of my heart be acceptable in your sight,
O LORD, my rock and my redeemer.

PSALM 19:14 ESV

Father, lately I've been obsessing over something. I can't stop thinking about it. At all. I've been obsessing so much over it that it could be considered an idol. Could You please help me readjust my thinking? I want to keep my eyes and focus on You. I want to! I'd like what my heart dwells on to be acceptable in Your sight—and that means not being consumed by the thoughts and concerns and desires of this world. As hard as it may be to readjust my thinking, I want to do it. Please help me. Please transform me by renewing my mind. In Jesus' name I pray, amen.

GOD IS FOR YOU!

What, then, shall we say in response to these things? If God is for us, who can be against us?

ROMANS 8:31 NIV

Father God, it is so good to be known and loved by You. I absolutely adore knowing that You are for me. And when You are for me, my Lord, no one else can be against me. Sure, it doesn't seem like everyone always likes me, but when it comes down to it, You're in control of all. You can and do change people's hearts. And You can and do change situations. I pray that I'll boldly trust You and live my faith out, knowing that I can be brave and follow Your leading. Thank You for the amazing way You care for me! In Jesus' name I pray, amen.

CREATED ON PURPOSE

*I will give thanks to You, for I am fearfully
and wonderfully made; wonderful are Your
works, and my soul knows it very well.*

PSALM 139:14 NASB

Lord God, in Your Word You say that I am fearfully
and wonderfully made. It means so much that You say
that, but often I don't believe that truth. Deep down,
I doubt it. I don't always like the way I look. Some
days I don't like my hair. Other days it's my face. And
I wish my body were different. Yet You have made me
just the way I am. As the Master Artist, You believe
I am beautiful. You created me to look like this for a
specific reason. When I'm tempted to be unhappy
with the way I look, please remind me that You see
me. You know me. And You love me—just the way I
am. Thank You for making me in an amazing and
wonderful way. In Jesus' name I pray, amen.

ALIVE!

But God, being rich in mercy, because of the great love with which he loved us, even when we were dead in our trespasses, made us alive together with Christ—by grace you have been saved.

EPHESIANS 2:4-5 ESV

Father, You are so absolutely rich with Your mercy. Mercy I don't deserve and mercy I can't earn. I thank You for that forgiveness and for Your grace— undeserved gifts that bring me to life in Christ. Thank You for saving me through Him. Thank You for loving me so very much, even when I was far from You and dead without Christ. Tonight, as I think about all that's happened in my day, I thank You that I can take some time to think about what really, truly matters: Your mercy and love and saving grace. Even when details of my life try to crowd out what's important, I can step back and appreciate You and Your great gifts to me. Thank You! In Jesus' name I pray, amen.

BUiLDiNG UP

*Therefore encourage one
another and build each other up.*
1 THESSALONIANS 5:11 NIV

Lord, sometimes I say and do things I don't want to say or do. I feel moody, and I don't always like what I think or say when I'm in a bad mood. I don't exactly know how to change. But I do know I want to be a bright spot in the lives of others. And I want to be a good example for You. When I'm tempted to tear other people down in my grumpiness, please stop my words—or help me change to words that build people up. When I'd rather disrespect my parents because they don't understand what I'm going through, please help me honor them with the words I say and my body language too. When I'd love to use a snappy but hurtful comeback, please shut the door of my mouth. Please transform my moods, words, thoughts, and actions so that they please You. In Jesus' name I pray, amen.

Do You Believe This?

*Jesus said to her, "I am the resurrection and the life.
Whoever believes in me, though he die, yet shall
he live, and everyone who lives and believes in
me shall never die. Do you believe this?"*

John 11:25–26 ESV

Jesus, I do believe You are the resurrection and the life! I am so thankful You came to earth so that people like me could believe in You and never die. And I'm thankful that all I need is to believe. I don't have to jump through a bunch of hoops or worry about doing a bunch of good works to earn my way to an eternity with You. Belief in You can be something so simple yet hard to actually do. But tonight, I want to affirm that I believe in You and thank You for the forever life You've promised. You are so good to me! I love You. In Your name I pray, amen.

SWEET SLEEP

In vain you rise early and stay up late,
toiling for food to eat—for he grants
sleep to those he loves.

PSALM 127:2 NIV

Lord God, I'm having such a hard time falling asleep tonight. When I toss and turn, it feels like I can't turn my brain off. I can't seem to stop thinking about what happened today or what could be coming in the future. Would You please quiet my thoughts? I pray that You'll grant me peace—peace that only comes from You. And in that peace, I pray I can find rest. Please help me rest peacefully tonight so I can wake up refreshed tomorrow morning, ready to serve and worship You. In Jesus' name I pray, amen.

ARE YOU WITH ME?

*The LORD was with Joseph and gave
him success in whatever he did.*

GENESIS 39:23 NIV

Father, Your Word is filled with great stories of what happened to men and women thousands of years ago. Even if it seems like ancient history to me, I can still learn valuable lessons from their lives and the ways You worked in and through them. I thank You that Joseph was a man who trusted You. It's so encouraging that You were with him no matter what. Even when he had every right to despair about his future—even when he was in prison—You were with him, giving him success. I may not be locked up in a prison, Lord, but I pray You'll be with me. Please bless what I say and do. Please give me success. In Jesus' name I pray, amen.

COME NEAR

*Come near to God and
he will come near to you.*
JAMES 4:8 NIV

Father God, I'm sorry I wander away from You so easily. I get distracted by the things of this world and the busyness of life. And while it shouldn't be an excuse, it's just what I do. Please forgive me. I want to come near to You. I wish I could cuddle up close to You and know You're there, caring for me. Father, in this moment tonight, I pray I'll feel You drawing me to You. I pray You'll fill my heart with Your peace and love. I would love to feel completely satisfied by You as I drift off to sleep. I love You and want to be able to shut out all the noise from this world and focus on You and You alone. I know You've given me all of Yourself through Your Son. How much of me do You have though? I pray I wouldn't be afraid to give You all of me—all that I have and all that I am. In Jesus' name I pray, amen.

TAMING MY TONGUE

*The one who has knowledge uses
words with restraint, and whoever
has understanding is even-tempered.*

PROVERBS 17:27 NIV

Lord Jesus, sometimes I wonder if it matters what I say. Are words really that important? But then I remember that You are the Word made flesh. You matter. And what You said matters. Similarly, what I say really does matter. Please help me watch what I say. When I'm tempted to blurt out every single thought that comes to mind, please help me learn to control my tongue. Please help me remember that I can and should honor You with my words. Please help me speak with restraint (even though it's so hard!). In Your name I pray, amen.

WHERE ARE YOU?

My God, I cry out by day, but you do
not answer, by night, but I find no rest.
PSALM 22:2 NIV

Father, I want to hear from You. Sometimes when I pray, it feels like my prayers are just bouncing back to me—like You don't hear them. Deep down, though, I know You hear. And deep down, I know You care. But it feels so discouraging to wait for an answer or some kind of guidance from You. I pray I will continue to trust in You even when it doesn't feel like You're there. I pray that You'll help me as I wait for You. Would You please give me peace as I trust and wait? As I long for You, I want to keep praying in faith. Morning and night and all throughout the day, I want to share with You what I'm feeling. Please help my faith grow stronger and stronger as I wait for You. In Jesus' name I pray, amen.

LET MY LIGHT SHINE

"You are the light of the world. A city set on a hill cannot be hidden. . . . In the same way, let your light shine before others, so that they may see your good works and give glory to your Father who is in heaven."

MATTHEW 5:14, 16 ESV

Lord Jesus, I'm so glad You came to this earth not just to save those who would believe in You but also to teach so much truth. At times it feels a little overwhelming to know that I'm a light in this world. And my light can't be hidden—because it's light! Light always drives away darkness, so I pray You'll use me as a light wherever I go. In school, at church, at my job, in my community, in my home—please help me faithfully stand up for what I believe in and what is true. Please help me keep in mind that where I am right now is temporary. I won't always be a teenager. I won't always be surrounded by the people I see every day. But my soul is eternal. Please help me live each day with this in mind. In Your name I pray, amen.

WORTH SO MUCH MORE

"Are not two sparrows sold for a penny? Yet not one of them will fall to the ground outside your Father's care. And even the very hairs of your head are all numbered. So don't be afraid; you are worth more than many sparrows."

MATTHEW 10:29–31 NIV

Father God, You are Alpha and Omega, Beginning and End. You are the Creator and Sustainer of all life. I am one girl in a sea of other girls—they seem countless to me, yet You know how many girls You've created. And You know how many strands of hair are on each and every head. The fact that You are all-knowing is awesome and amazing. It's also a little scary! But I come to You humbled with a well-deserved fear and honor of You. I'm not worthy of Your mercy, but You've lavished me with it anyway. I'm in awe of how generous You are and how Your love and forgiveness are such undeserved gifts of favor. Thank You. You are a good, good God! In Jesus' name I pray, amen.

WHATEVER you DO

And whatever you do, whether in word or deed,
do it all in the name of the Lord Jesus, giving
thanks to God the Father through him.

<small>COLOSSIANS 3:17 NIV</small>

Father God, I want to honor You in everything I do and say—and I want people to be able to see Jesus living in me. I admit this isn't always easy. Sometimes I struggle to remember to watch what I say. If You need to, Lord, please keep a door over my mouth. . . and don't hesitate to shut it. If that's what it takes to keep me from saying things that don't glorify You, then I'm willing. I thank You, Father, for the voice You've given me. Please help me use it to share Your love and kindness with the world. And thank You for the ability to do things for You. Please use me to reach this world for You! In Jesus' name I pray, amen.

SHINE LIKE STARS

Do everything without grumbling or arguing,
so that you may become blameless and pure,
"children of God without fault in a warped
and crooked generation." Then you will
shine among them like stars in the sky as
you hold firmly to the word of life.

PHILIPPIANS 2:14–16 NIV

Father God, tonight I confess that it's really easy to spend a lot of time grumbling and complaining. But every time I do, I end up being critical. I only spend time looking for what's wrong or annoying, and I shut my eyes to what's really good around me. I miss out on Your good gifts when all I do is find fault with things. I want to be without fault in this crooked generation. I want to live like Your child and shine like a star in the sky. To do that, I need to give up my tendency to grumble. I need to hold on to Your Word of life and let that shine through what I say, do, and think about. In Jesus' name I pray, amen.

A NEW THING

*"Forget the former things; do not dwell
on the past. See, I am doing a new thing!
Now it springs up; do you not perceive it?"*

Isaiah 43:18–19 NIV

Father, I praise You for being God Almighty, full of power. I know I should try to be content with where You have me in life—because You have a purpose and a plan. But sometimes I wish I could have a fresh start. I feel stuck right now, but I trust that someday You'll bring changes into my life. Please guide me to a new start. Help me make wise choices that glorify You. And when changes do come and I realize I have a new beginning, please help me remember where I've come from. I pray that I won't dwell on the past, but at the same time, I don't want to forget where You've brought me and what You've done in my life. I love You, Lord! In Jesus' name I pray, amen.

YOU ARE MY TRUST

For you, O Lord, are my hope,
my trust, O LORD, from my youth.
PSALM 71:5 ESV

Lord, sometimes I wonder how I can trust You. But then the bigger question is this: How could I not trust You? You're completely worthy of my trust. With hope, I expect You and Your promises with complete confidence. What would my life be like without You? I'm thankful I know You and can rest in You from my youth. Oh, how empty my life would be without Your guidance! Who or what would I trust in if it wasn't for You? Thank You for keeping Your promises and being trustworthy. In Jesus' name I pray, amen.

MY POWERFUL GOD

*"He did this so that all the peoples of
the earth might know that the hand
of the LORD is powerful and so that you
might always fear the LORD your God."*

JOSHUA 4:24 NIV

Father God, all throughout history, You've made a
way for Your people. You protect and provide for
Your children. Your hand has worked powerfully in
the lives of those who believe in You, including mine.
I know the great things You have done for me—things
I never could have done for myself. You've treated
me with so much kindness and favor. Thank You! I
pray I'll remember the way You've so faithfully and
lovingly provided for me. You are all-powerful. You
always have been, and You always will be. With
You as my Lord and my God, who is there on earth
I can fear? I praise You for how perfect You are and
thank You for Your loving care each day of my life.
In Jesus' name I pray, amen.

FOLLOWING YOUR LEAD

By faith Abraham obeyed when he was
called to go out to a place that he was to
receive as an inheritance. And he went out,
not knowing where he was going.

HEBREWS 11:8 ESV

Father God, You have had a special relationship with certain people throughout history. You are close with those who are faithful to You. When I look at the life of Abraham in Genesis, You asked him to do a huge thing—trust You with the unknown. You asked him to trust You by leaving his home and following You. Instead of letting his heart and decisions be influenced by what was comfortable and familiar, he chose to step out in faith and obey You. He had no idea where You would lead him; he only knew You would lead him. Just like Abraham, I pray that I'll be ready and willing to follow where You'll lead me, even when it seems scary or uncertain. As I look to my future, I pray I'll follow Your guidance and not be afraid to boldly do all that You ask me. Please make my way abundantly clear. In Jesus' name I pray, amen.

WISHING AND HOPING

Many are the plans in a person's heart,
but it is the LORD's purpose that prevails.
PROVERBS 19:21 NIV

Father God, You know that I have so many dreams for my future, and even some plans that will hopefully make my wishes a reality. I know what I'd like to have happen in my life. But ultimately, Your purpose is what will unfold. You have plans for me and things I need to experience and face. I want to trust You. Please help me welcome Your will for me. If I need to change my hopes and dreams and plans to go along with Your purpose for me, please help me be open to change. I'm so excited to see what You're going to do in my life and through me! In Jesus' name I pray, amen.

LEAD ME

The LORD is my shepherd, I lack nothing. He makes me lie down in green pastures, he leads me beside quiet waters, he refreshes my soul. He guides me along the right paths for his name's sake.

PSALM 23:1–3 NIV

Father, when I look at the world around me, I wonder how much longer this world will even exist. You've promised that Jesus will return—but I'm afraid I won't know when He does. How will I know? Your Word says that many will come claiming they're the Christ. But Your Word also promises that Your sheep—Your children!—will know their Shepherd's voice. Please help my heart know Your voice. I love Jesus. He is my Shepherd. I pray He will lead me and that I'll faithfully listen to Him and follow. I'm so thankful He gives me all I need. Please help me rest in the fact that I am Yours, and You won't lead me astray. In Jesus' name I pray, amen.

WISE FRIENDS

Whoever walks with the wise becomes wise,
but the companion of fools will suffer harm.
<small>PROVERBS 13:20 ESV</small>

Lord, sometimes it's hard for me to remember how important it is to choose my friends wisely. It's tempting to try to fit in with the popular crowd—or at least a bunch of friends who want to spend time with me. But instead of focusing so much on what's on the outside, please help me to see what my "friends" really are like. Are they leading me away from You? Are they influencing me to do things that are sinful or just not very healthy for me? As much as I want to have friends, I don't want to back down on what I know to be right. I pray I would make right, holy choices. If my friends can't help me do that, I pray You'll bring other friends into my life. I'd love to become wise—and definitely not be a fool. Please keep me from making foolish friend choices. In Jesus' name I pray, amen.

WALKING IN THE LIGHT

But if we walk in the light, as he is in the light,
we have fellowship with one another, and the
blood of Jesus his Son cleanses us from all sin.

1 JOHN 1:7 ESV

Father, I know what it's like to be scared of the dark. Nighttime can be spooky just because I can't see what's out there. When I was younger, the darkness seemed even more threatening; nightlights and flash-lights were helpful because the light drove away darkness. Just like the dark of night is less scary when there's light, it's much easier to walk through my life with Your light. I am so thankful Jesus is the Light of the World. I'm thankful I know Him. I'm thankful for the way Your Word is a lamp to my feet and a light for my path. And I'm thankful I don't have to stumble through the darkness of the world on my own because You light the way. I want to keep walking in Your light. In Jesus' name I pray, amen.

THE MOMENT

"Very truly I tell you, whoever hears my word and believes him who sent me has eternal life and will not be judged but has crossed over from death to life."

JOHN 5:24 NIV

Father, for You, belief is the dividing line between eternal life and eternal death. But I haven't always believed in You. In fact, there definitely was a time in my life when I didn't. So my very big, important question tonight is this: Have I believed in You? And when was the moment I chose to believe in Christ and trust my eternal destination with Him? If I've never said it before, Lord, I do believe in You! I believe You sent Jesus. And I trust my eternity with Him. I want to cross over from death to life. It's in Jesus' name I pray, amen.

CREATED FOR GOOD WORKS

*For we are His workmanship, created in Christ
Jesus for good works, which God prepared
beforehand so that we would walk in them.*

EPHESIANS 2:10 NASB

Father, I'm blown away that You created me for good works—and that You've already prepared them for me! I really wish I could skip ahead and see what they are, but I'll try to wait patiently as You reveal Your plan and purposes over time. It's amazing that You care for me so much and have a plan for my life. Please help me have courage and faith to follow Your leading and do all of the good works You have for me. Please use me in an amazing way. In Jesus' name I pray, amen.

LIVING BY HIS WORD

Be diligent to present yourself approved to God
as a workman who does not need to be ashamed,
accurately handling the word of truth.

2 TIMOTHY 2:15 NASB

Thank You for Your Word, Lord. Thank You that it's true. Thank You that I can base my life on it. I pray that I could accurately handle Your Word. I pray I'd know it more. Help me find ways to study and memorize it. I pray it will transform my heart, my mind, and my entire life. As it works in my heart, I want it to show in my life. I don't want to be ashamed when You see my life. More than anything, I want You to approve of what I think and say and do. Please help me live a life pleasing to You. In Your name I pray, amen.

A TRUSTWORTHY TEEN

A gossip betrays a confidence, but a
trustworthy person keeps a secret.
PROVERBS 11:13 NIV

Father God, You created all things, including my mouth and my tongue. I can use my mouth and tongue to tell others about You and bring healing and life. Or I can use them to hurt and destroy. When I choose to open my mouth and talk about other people, usually it's hurtful. I pray I'll learn to keep my mouth shut when I should. I pray I'll become a trustworthy girl—worthy of the trust of others—and keep secrets when asked. I pray that I'll grow into a respectable, responsible woman, who knows when to speak and when to keep silent. I want to build people up with my words. Please help me think before I speak. In Jesus' name I pray, amen.

THE APPLE OF YOUR EYE

Keep me as the apple of your eye;
hide me in the shadow of your wings from
the wicked who are out to destroy me,
from my mortal enemies who surround me.

PSALM 17:8–9 NIV

Father God, You are my protector. You know me and keep me safe. I thank You for the way You hide me in the shadow of Your wings. When I imagine how a mama bird cares for her young and would do anything to protect her babies, I know the same is true for You. You're always alert, always protecting me, always watching out for my best. Thank You. Thank You that I don't have to live in fear of what people will try to do to me. Thank You that even though enemies try to destroy me—sometimes quite literally—You're the One who protects me. I pray You'll continue to keep me as the apple of Your eye. In Jesus' name I pray, amen.

SOMETHING SPECIAL

*But you are a chosen people, a royal priesthood,
a holy nation, God's special possession, that you
may declare the praises of him who called you
out of darkness into his wonderful light.*

1 PETER 2:9 NIV

Father, to know that You have chosen me is almost too much to comprehend. I don't understand why You chose me, but I'm so thankful You did. Please help me remember that because of Jesus' sacrifice, I am royal and holy. Let me live like I am with all that I choose to say and do. Remind me how I am a princess—the daughter of the King of kings. As a special possession of the Most High God, I pray that I'll boldly proclaim your excellencies. Thank You for calling me out of the darkness and into Your marvelous light. Please help me be a light to my friends and family who still are living in darkness. In Jesus' name I pray, amen.

WITHOUT SIN

Who can say, "I have kept my heart pure; I am clean and without sin"?

PROVERBS 20:9 NIV

Father, when I look around me, I see so much wrong in the world. So much sin. And people celebrate their sin. It's wrong. And I know it grieves Your heart to see. You sent Jesus into this world to save all who fall short of Your perfection, if they'd just recognize Him as Lord. Thank You for sending Him. And thank You for opening my eyes and heart to accept Him and the sacrifice He made for me. Please forgive my sins, and help me not to think of myself higher than I should. Please remind me that without Jesus, I'm a sinner like everyone else around me. Please help me take Jesus into the world. Help me reach people You bring into my life with the good news of Jesus. In His name I pray, amen.

CHOOSE KINDNESS

*If you really keep the royal law found in Scripture,
"Love your neighbor as yourself," you are doing
right. But if you show favoritism, you sin and are
convicted by the law as lawbreakers.*

JAMES 2:8–9 NIV

Father, You've created all people. But why are some
people so mean? I know that You created man, and
since the Garden of Eden, people have turned away
from You to go their own ways. In the days of Noah,
the wickedness of men grieved Your heart—and it
still does. So when people are nasty today, it's not
what makes You happy. It breaks my heart when
people say or do hurtful things. And other girls who
purposefully exclude me crush my spirit. Please help
me look past the mean things people have said or
done to me. Please help me to not look to them or
their approval for my worth. Please help me remember that my value is in You. And please help me treat
others without favoritism. I want to be kind and loving
to everyone. In Jesus' name I pray, amen.

CLEAN HANDS AND A PURE HEART

The one who has clean hands and a pure heart,
who does not trust in an idol or swear by a false
god. They will receive blessing from the LORD.

PSALM 24:4–5 NIV

Father, I confess that at times I'm tempted to cheat. To me, it might seem minor, like just fudging a little bit or peeking at information I shouldn't see or making sure things work out in my favor. In Your eyes, though, these kinds of efforts to get ahead are wrong. They're sinful—they miss the mark of what You've called me to as Your daughter. Lord, I confess my guilt. I pray You'll forgive me, help me repent and turn away from these habits, and wipe my conscience clean. I want to do what's right in Your eyes. I want to have clean hands and a pure heart. I don't want to be false or deceitful. In Jesus' name I pray, amen.

TALK ABOUT IT

But in your hearts honor Christ the Lord as holy, always being prepared to make a defense to anyone who asks you for a reason for the hope that is in you; yet do it with gentleness and respect.

1 PETER 3:15 ESV

Lord Jesus, I want to honor You in my heart and remember that, as much as You're my forever friend, You're holy. With that always in mind, I pray I'll be ready to talk about what You've done in my life. When people ask me why I have hope or make certain choices, please help me to gently tell about You. I don't want to scare people away from You, but I also don't want to be so shy that I keep my love for You hidden. I pray I'll be able to talk about You clearly while respecting whomever I'm talking with. I pray it will feel natural to talk about You and how You've worked in my life. In Your name I pray, amen.

MERCY!

But when the kindness of God our Savior and
His love for mankind appeared, He saved us,
not on the basis of deeds which we have done
in righteousness, but according to His mercy.

TITUS 3:4–5 NASB

Lord God, You are so kind! As much as people wonder where You are when bad things happen, I see Your kindness and goodness all around me. You loved people so much that You made a way for us to be right with You. Through Your mercy, You saved us! You knew we couldn't be righteous on our own. And there's no deed I must do to earn righteousness or a right standing with You. All I need to do is believe and welcome Your mercy. Tonight, I do. I believe in You. And I'm thankful for the way You've saved me with mercy I'll never deserve. In Jesus' name I pray, amen.

HOLY AND BLAMELESS

*He chose us in Him before the foundation
of the world, that we would be holy
and blameless before Him.*

EPHESIANS 1:4 NASB

Father God, I'm amazed that You would choose me before You even created the world. Me! I'm chosen. It's a concept that seems so strange—yet I'm forever grateful. Thank You for adopting me and bringing me into Your family. Thank You for Your undeserved favor so that I would and could be holy and blameless before You, the one and only holy and blameless God. You are kind. I can do nothing that would make me deserve this precious grace, so I come to You tonight to thank You. I love You! In Jesus' name I pray, amen.

A NEW CREATION

Therefore if anyone is in Christ, he is
a new creature; the old things passed
away; behold, new things have come.

2 CORINTHIANS 5:17 NASB

Father God, thank You for the gift of new beginnings. I love the fact that when I believed and trusted in Christ, I became a new creation. Everything in my past—all of the old things that alienated me and kept me from You—is dead and gone. You've brought new, wonderful things. Thank You for taking all that's old and wiping it away. Thank You for making all things new. I pray that I'll fall asleep tonight resting in this beautiful truth. I am a new creation in Christ! In His name I pray, amen.

PEACE THAT I CAN'T UNDERSTAND

And the peace of God, which surpasses all understanding, will guard your hearts and your minds in Christ Jesus.

PHILIPPIANS 4:7 ESV

Father, I'm glad that I can come to You at any time and be completely honest with You—because I feel so stressed out right now. I feel like I'm under so much pressure. And I want to do my best. I want things to go well. Please help me remember that I can rest in You. Jesus promised that His yoke was easy and His burden was light. Mine feels difficult and heavy. Please help me to take on His yoke and burden, not my own. As I give You my burdens, I pray You'll fill me with a deep peace that I can't explain or fully understand. Your peace, oh Lord, would be so wonderful right now! And to know that Your peace will guard my heart and mind brings such a comfort and relief. Thank You! In Jesus' name I pray, amen.

IT'S A GOOD DAY!

*When times are good, be happy; but when
times are bad, consider this: God has
made the one as well as the other.*

ECCLESIASTES 7:14 NIV

Father God, there are good days and bad days—and today I'm thankful for all of the very good things You've done. For the little great things and best parts of today, I thank You. For the parts where I needed to trust You a little more, I'm thankful. For the moments You surprised me with Your faithfulness, I'm grateful. For the way You've poured out Your love and favor, I'm humbled. I love You, Lord, no matter what. But when You thrill me with good things, it really makes my day. Thank You! In Jesus' name I pray, amen.

FORGIVEN

*If we confess our sins, he is faithful and just
and will forgive us our sins and purify
us from all unrighteousness.*

1 JOHN 1:9 NIV

Father God, I come to You tonight knowing how I've sinned against You today. Of course, I'm never perfect because everyone sins and no one qualifies for Your glory. But I know there's forgiveness. I just have to confess how I've sinned. And so I do. Please search my heart. And please forgive me for my mistakes. I pray I won't fall into the same traps tomorrow. Please help me make right, pure choices. Please help me turn away from sin. Thank You for being faithful and just. And, Lord, thank You so much for Your forgiveness! I don't deserve it, but I'm so thankful for it. In Jesus' name I pray, amen.

FLAWLESS

"Every word of God is flawless; he is a
shield to those who take refuge in him."
PROVERBS 30:5 NIV

Father God, thank You for Your Word. Thank You that it's true. Thank You that it's flawless. Thank You that it's timeless. As Your way of communicating with me, I love the way it leads me. I'm thankful that it can protect me—not only in the way it guides me to live a wise, holy life but also in the way that it leads me to salvation. Instead of relying on catchy phrases or beliefs that are popular right now, please help me stay firmly grounded in You and Your Word. You give me so much protection. You are my shield, and Your Word is the sword of the Spirit, the weapon I can use to defend myself every day. I pray that I'll hide Your Word in my heart and let it change my life. In Jesus' name I pray, amen.

TRANSFORMED!

*Do not conform to the pattern of this world,
but be transformed by the renewing of your mind.
Then you will be able to test and approve what
God's will is—his good, pleasing and perfect will.*

ROMANS 12:2 NIV

Father God, this world and the desires and goals of this world are so different from You and Your will. I pray I wouldn't try to shove myself into the mold of what's "normal" or desirable in the world. Instead, I pray You'll transform me. Please renew my mind so I can discern what Your will is. I want to do Your will because it's good, pleasing, and perfect. Things in this world are so imperfect. I pray I'll carefully judge my options every day and choose to honor and please You with what I do and say. In Jesus' name I pray, amen.

NO SHAME

I trust in you; do not let me be put to shame,
nor let my enemies triumph over me.

PSALM 25:2 NIV

Father, thank You for loving me no matter what.
And thank You for always being with me. Tonight I
really need some time with You, remembering who I
am in You. I was so embarrassed today. Sometimes
I don't know why I say the things I do or act the way
I do. And I don't always like what happens to me.
Honestly, some days and weeks it's rare that I do like
what happens. But even in all of my embarrassment
and discontentment, please help me remember that
You can work things for my good. You can use these
uncomfortable, unwanted moments to turn me into
a woman who trusts You for all. In Jesus' name I
pray, amen.

SO LONELY

I lie awake, I have become like
a lonely bird on a housetop.
PSALM 102:7 NASB

Father, I thank You that You're always with me. I know You are. But sometimes it's so hard to keep that in mind because I'm lonely. I try to fill that loneliness with other things. I might want to fill it with a boyfriend. Sometimes I think better or different friends would take my loneliness away. But none of those relationships will really fill my loneliness. Things won't fill it either—not food, not shopping, not social media approval, not being busy with activities, not working hard to get good grades. Only You can fill the void I feel. Even if I don't always know exactly what I feel, only You can satisfy what I'm missing. I pray I can rest in that, especially when I'm feeling alone. In Jesus' name I pray, amen.

MY IMPERFECT BEST

*Whatever you do, work at it with all
your heart, as working for the Lord, not for
human masters, since you know that you
will receive an inheritance from the Lord as a
reward. It is the Lord Christ you are serving.*
Colossians 3:23–24 NIV

Lord Jesus, it really is an honor to serve You. I pray that every day I'll wake up and remember that I'm here to work for You—not for my parents, not for my teachers, not for a coach. But in all that I do, I want to do my best. Lord, I'm sorry that my best isn't perfect. In fact, sometimes I wonder if I should even try since what I do seems so imperfect. Please help me remember that You've never called me to perfection. Perfection is impossible for anyone but You! Even when perfection won't be my reality, I pray I'll still do things with all my heart, whether it's my schoolwork or hobbies or chores or even the way I spend time with people around me. It's an honor and gift to serve You, and I pray I'll think of everything I do as a service to You. In Your name I pray, amen.

GROWiNG UP

*Rather, speaking the truth in love,
we are to grow up in every way into
him who is the head, into Christ.*

EPHESIANS 4:15 ESV

Father, thank You for drawing me close to You before I'm an adult. Even though it feels like it might take a long time to break out and be on my own, I know I've grown up pretty quickly so far. In fact, in a lot of ways, it feels like my time as a little girl passed by quickly. Sometimes I think it would be nice to be a little girl again, when life was easier and I didn't have so many concerns and huge choices to make. Please help me remember that You'll always be my Abba Father—my Daddy! Also, please give me courage to grow up in You. I want to know You more and more every day and become a woman whose entire heart is set on You. In Jesus' name I pray, amen.

LiGHT iNSTEAD Of DARKNESS

*When Jesus spoke again to the people,
he said, "I am the light of the world.
Whoever follows me will never walk in
darkness, but will have the light of life."*

JOHN 8:12 NIV

Lord Jesus, You are the Light of the World! I'm thankful that because of You I don't have to walk in darkness. Thank You for giving me the light of life. When darkness and fear threaten to steal my focus, I pray that I'll keep my mind on You. Thanks for the amazing ways You light my path. If I stick with You and stop trying to go my own way, You'll lead me moment by moment. I may not know what's coming up, but You do. And as long as I stick with You, You'll make everything clear. That brings me so much comfort, and for that I'm thankful. In Your name I pray, amen.

NO FEAR iN DEATH

Since the children have flesh and blood,
he [Jesus] too shared in their humanity so
that by his death he might break the power
of him who holds the power of death—that is,
the devil—and free those who all their lives
were held in slavery by their fear of death.

HEBREWS 2:14–15 NIV

Father God, death is such an awful thing. When someone close to me dies, it feels like my heart is breaking. I want to talk to, see, and hug my loved one, but I can't. You know death is awful. And You thought it was so awful that You made a way out—so death doesn't have the final say and it doesn't need to be feared. Because You sent Jesus to earth as a man, His death and life after death broke the power of death. Thank You that for those who believe in Your Son, there's life after death. There's hope. Please help me focus on that hope, and comfort me as I grieve. In Jesus' name I pray, amen.

WHOM WILL YOU SERVE?

"Now fear the LORD and serve him with all faithfulness. Throw away the gods your ancestors worshiped beyond the Euphrates River and in Egypt, and serve the LORD. But if serving the LORD seems undesirable to you, then choose for yourselves this day whom you will serve."

JOSHUA 24:14–15 NIV

Father God, the older I get the more I want to stretch my wings and be more independent. I want to make my own decisions instead of being told what to do. I want some freedom to figure out who I really am. Yet with all of my desires to be independent, part of me also is really scared. What if I make a wrong choice? What if my decisions lead to something really bad? Please help me make choices that will glorify You and bring You honor. I choose to serve You. As long as I do that, I don't have to be afraid. And I'll know that You can use my independence and choices for You. In Jesus' name I pray, amen.

MAKING FUTURE PLANS

Come now, you who say, "Today or tomorrow we will go into such and such a town and spend a year there and trade and make a profit"—yet you do not know what tomorrow will bring. What is your life? For you are a mist that appears for a little time and then vanishes. Instead you ought to say, "If the Lord wills, we will live and do this or that."

JAMES 4:13–15 ESV

Father, I admit that I like to try to plan ahead. I'd love to know what will happen in my future. It's fun to imagine and prepare for what might happen to me. So often, I bank a lot on my future. But I need to remember that You're in charge of tomorrow. I have no idea what will happen! Instead of making all kinds of big plans, please help me focus on today. I want to trust You with my future and do the things You'd have me do. I want to do Your will. Please help me surrender my desires and instead focus on serving You and accomplishing Your will for me each day. In Jesus' name I pray, amen.

WHY DO I NEED DISCIPLINE?

*Whoever heeds discipline shows the
way to life, but whoever ignores
correction leads others astray.*

PROVERBS 10:17 NIV

Father, I have to admit that discipline doesn't seem
so great to me. When I think of discipline, I think of
something I've done wrong—or some strict set of
rules I need to follow. But if I would stop thinking
about how much I don't like the thought of discipline
and just pay attention to what You ask of me, my life
would be better. When it comes down to it, I don't
want to ignore Your correction. Deep down, I know
You correct and discipline me because You love
me and want what's best for me. Please help me
remember this and listen to Your direction. In Jesus'
name I pray, amen.

MY LiGHT

*The LORD is my light and my salvation; whom shall
I fear? The LORD is the stronghold of my
life; of whom shall I be afraid?*

PSALM 27:1 ESV

Jesus, when You came to earth You called Yourself the Light of the World. That's exactly what You are! Just thinking of You and how much You love me lights my darkest days. I don't have to fear anything or anyone because of You. You have saved me. You brighten my darkness. And I can trust You absolutely and completely with all of me. When the worries of this world seem to pile up and I'm tempted to feel overwhelmed, I pray for peace to flood my heart. Please help me remember that I don't need to fear anything or anyone. You light my way. You've saved me. Thank You. In Your name I pray, amen.

FRiEND OF THE WORLD?
OR A FRiEND OF GOD?

You adulterous people! Do you not know that friendship with the world is enmity with God? Therefore whoever wishes to be a friend of the world makes himself an enemy of God.

JAMES 4:4 ESV

Father God, tonight I apologize to You for trying to be a friend of the world. I'm sorry for the times when I lose sight of You and Your plans and purposes. Instead, I focus on things that don't matter: popularity, clothing, my appearance, relationships, and what others think of me. Instead of trying to be a people pleaser, I want to please You. I don't want my thoughts to be consumed with things of this world. I don't want to spend all my time thinking about what I have or don't have. I don't want to spend my life figuring out how to be accepted by this world. And I definitely don't want to be Your enemy. I love You! I want my life to please You. And I want to be Your friend. In Jesus' name I pray, amen.

ALWAYS WITH ME

How precious to me are your thoughts,
O God! How vast is the sum of them!
If I would count them, they are more than
the sand. I awake, and I am still with you.

PSALM 139:17-18 ESV

Father God, I'm truly amazed by You. You are so much bigger and more powerful than anything I can imagine or comprehend. And You know all. All things! I praise You for the things You think and plan and bring into action. I praise You for being all-knowing and always present. Thank You for never sleeping and never letting me out of Your thoughts. No matter what I do—whether I'm sleeping or I'm awake—I'm with You. You'll never leave me. That is such a comfort. I pray I'll fall asleep tonight resting in that wonderful truth. In Jesus' name I pray, amen.

UNDER PRESSURE

"Keep watching and praying that you may not enter into temptation; the spirit is willing, but the flesh is weak."

MATTHEW 26:41 NASB

Father, I had a hard time today. Someone was pressuring me to do something I know I shouldn't do. The thing is, the temptation seemed pretty appealing. As much as I know I shouldn't give in, part of me wants to. What should I do, Lord? I know You'll never leave me, no matter what. But because You love me and because I love You, I want to make You happy. And I know obedience to You will make You happy. Please help me not give in to temptation. I might feel so weak, but I want to obey You. Please help me stay strong. In Jesus' name I pray, amen.

WALK iN LOVE

*And walk in love, as Christ loved us
and gave himself up for us, a fragrant
offering and sacrifice to God.*

EPHESIANS 5:2 ESV

Father, Your Word tells me that You are love. When Jesus was on earth, He commanded His disciples to love each other as He had loved them. I know I need to love others. Sometimes I want to love other people, but other times I don't. Please help me do it! Tomorrow, please open my eyes and show me how I can walk in Your love. I'll admit that it feels like a sacrifice to love people I don't want to love—or to love people I may not even think deserve my love. Please help me love them anyway. Give me eyes to see people around me who need Your love, then give me the strength and courage to love them well. In Jesus' name I pray, amen.

SHOW ME THE WAY

"I am the LORD your God, who teaches you what is best for you, who directs you in the way you should go. If only you had paid attention to my commands, your peace would have been like a river, your well-being like the waves of the sea."

ISAIAH 48:17–18 NIV

Father, I love that You always know what's happening—what has happened, is happening, and will happen in the future. And I love that You have a plan not just for the world but for me and my life too. Knowing that You have a plan for my future helps me rest in You. Sometimes I get so scared I'm not doing the right things, or I get confused when I need to make wise choices that affect my life. I want to pay attention to Your commands and do Your will. I want to do all that You have planned for me! I'm willing. Please use me. In whatever way, please give me opportunities, strength, and courage to do all You call me to do. I'm excited to be used by You through the power of Your Holy Spirit. In Jesus' name I pray, amen.

BECOMING A PEACEMAKER

"Blessed are the peacemakers, for they will be called children of God."

MATTHEW 5:9 NIV

Lord Jesus, You brought peace to this world through Your life and Your death. And You've brought peace to me! I pray I would model Your peace in this world. Please help me live peacefully with the people around me. Instead of stirring up trouble, I want to be a calming influence. Even when people would rather lash out in anger or hate, I pray I'll still give peaceful responses. If I try to bring peace to a situation, please help me know that's all You ask of me. My peace may not be received well, but I can still try. Like You, I can offer peace no matter what. Not everyone accepts Your peace, yet You still offer it. I'll gladly take Your peace with a thankful heart. I love You, Jesus. In Your name I pray, amen.

HELP!

In my distress I called upon the LORD,
and cried to my God for help; He heard
my voice out of His temple, and my cry
for help before Him came into His ears.

PSALM 18:6 NASB

My Lord and my God, I need Your help. You know what's happening to me. I want to change what has happened, and truly, I'm afraid of what will happen. I don't want to live in fear though. And I don't want to live a life of regret. I need Your help. Thank You for listening to me. Thank You for knowing what I need before a word is even out of my mouth—and when I have no words to describe what I'm thinking and feeling. Thank You for hearing my cry for help. I'm so thankful for You and the way I can trust You completely. In Jesus' name I pray, amen.

WHAT I DON'T HAVE

The LORD will give strength to His people;
the LORD will bless His people with peace.

PSALM 29:11 NASB

Father God, tonight I come to You with so much on my mind. Even though it feels like my thoughts are weighing me down, I'm really thankful that You can change my worries to peace. You have a way of blessing me with peace like nothing else—and for that, I'm so glad. I'm also glad that You give strength. I know my weaknesses, but amazingly, Your power is perfected in my weakness. When I'm weak, You make me strong. It's incredible that You take what I'm lacking and then turn it into something great. When I'm tempted to get discouraged, I pray that You'll help me to keep my eyes on You and remember that You alone can help. I'm so thankful for You and Your peace and strength! In Jesus' name I pray, amen.

ONE STEP AT A TIME

Ponder the path of your feet; then all your ways will be sure. Do not swerve to the right or to the left; turn your foot away from evil.

PROVERBS 4:26–27 ESV

Father, thank You for today. I give tomorrow to You. Please use me how You'd like. As I make little and big decisions each moment, help me ponder the way I go. I don't want to just wander around and do or react to whatever comes my way. Please help me stay on the right path—the one You've planned for me. Please steer me away from evil. I want to live in a way that points others to You. As I try to do that, please show me what that way is. Please make my footsteps—and all of my choices—firm. In Jesus' name I pray, amen.

FREEDOM!

*Live as people who are free, not using
your freedom as a cover-up for evil,
but living as servants of God.*

1 PETER 2:16 ESV

Heavenly Father, thank You for freedom that comes through Jesus. I don't have to live as a slave to the law. I don't have to try to earn salvation on my own. I can't save myself, no matter what I do. Instead of feeling bad about that, I'm thankful that You've given me freedom. Thank You for saving me! As I enjoy my freedom in Christ, I pray that I won't use it as an excuse to sin and ask for forgiveness afterward. Instead, I want to live as Your servant. With thankfulness for the freedom that comes through You, I pray that I'll make choices that point to You. I don't want to waste my freedom, take it for granted, or misuse it. Please help me treat it as the incredible gift that it is. Thank You for Your true freedom. In Jesus' name I pray, amen.

LOVE IS THE ANSWER

"You have heard that it was said, 'Love your neighbor and hate your enemy.' But I tell you, love your enemies and pray for those who persecute you, that you may be children of your Father in heaven."

MATTHEW 5:43–45 NIV

Lord Jesus, your instruction to love my enemies and pray for those who persecute me is so difficult. It just doesn't feel natural to love people who are hurtful and filled with hate. But I choose to trust You, and I want to obey You. So as difficult as it may seem, please help me love people who enjoy being my enemies. When I'm tempted to respond out of hurt and fear, please help me to choose love. Please help me stand up against what's natural—hating my enemy—and be different from the world around me. Please help me live like I am a child of my Father in heaven. In Jesus' name I pray, amen.

THREE STUMBLING BLOCKS

*For all that is in the world—the desires of the flesh
and the desires of the eyes and pride of life—is
not from the Father but is from the world. And the
world is passing away along with its desires, but
whoever does the will of God abides forever.*

1 JOHN 2:16–17 ESV

Father God, it's really easy to be swayed by what's in the world: the desires of my flesh, the desires of my eyes, and the pride of life. All of what tempts me and so often consumes my thoughts falls into those three categories. Am I obsessing over relationships or how someone else can make me feel? Am I stuck thinking about what I want—either to buy or to have or to work toward? Or am I just proud of myself and all the things I do? Please help me remember that all of that isn't important. It will pass away—and vanish. Everything apart from You will be gone forever. I don't want to be stuck dwelling on what won't last or what's not important. In Jesus' name I pray, amen.

SETTING MY BODY APART

It is God's will that you should be sanctified: that
you should avoid sexual immorality; that each of
you should learn to control your own body in a way
that is holy and honorable, not in passionate lust
like the pagans, who do not know God. . . . For God
did not call us to be impure, but to live a holy life.

1 THESSALONIANS 4:3–5, 7 NIV

Father, so much in this world screams with immorality. People try to talk me into thinking or doing things that compromise my purity. It's hard to stay set apart—to follow Your desire for me to stay sanctified. I pray I would be set apart from the world and choose to control my body. In the heat of the moment, it can seem easier or more enjoyable to give in and do what I know I shouldn't do. I pray You'll give me the strength and wisdom to stop. Please keep me from impure choices and help me live a holy, self-controlled life. In Jesus' name I pray, amen.

WALK iN THE LiGHT

Let no one deceive you with empty words,
for because of these things the wrath of God
comes upon the sons of disobedience. Therefore
do not become partners with them; for at one
time you were darkness, but now you are light
in the Lord. Walk as children of light.

EPHESIANS 5:6–8 ESV

Father God, I don't want to be deceived! Deception seems awful to me, and I don't want empty words to lead me astray. I don't want to fall into a trap of believing one thing only to find out it's a lie. Instead, I want to walk in Your light and Your truth. I want it to be obvious that I'm a child of light. I pray I'll make choices that honor You. Please help me be careful with who I spend time with, and keep me from becoming partners with unbelievers. I want to be a light to people living in darkness without becoming like them. I pray that while I'm living in this world, I'll be set apart—not living like I'm holier than everyone else but making obedient choices that please You. In Jesus' name I pray, amen.

THE POWER OF CHOICE

God "will repay each person according to
what they have done." To those who by persistence
in doing good seek glory, honor and immortality,
he will give eternal life. But for those who are
self-seeking and who reject the truth and follow
evil, there will be wrath and anger.

ROMANS 2:6–8 NIV

Father, every day I'm faced with so many decisions. It's easy to make a choice in the heat of the moment and forget that it means something—and that it carries consequences. Please help me remember that You'll repay me according to what I do in this life. I want to persistently honor You. I want to bring You glory in all that I do. I want to live by the power of Your Holy Spirit. Please help me live like every moment matters. I pray that I'd look to the good of others and not just my own interests. I want to know Your truth and follow it, and I want it to obviously show in my life. Please help me keep my eyes on You. In Jesus' name I pray, amen.

LIVING IN PEACE

*Make every effort to live in peace
with everyone and to be holy.*

HEBREWS 12:14 NIV

Lord Jesus, You know how difficult it is to live in peace with everyone! Some people on this earth are difficult to get along with. And some people love to stir up trouble. It doesn't matter if it involves lying or fighting—they just want to tear other people down. I don't want to be like that, Lord. As much as it's in my control, I want to be a peacemaker. Please help me live in peace with everyone. Even when it's difficult, I pray I'll still try my hardest to bring peace to situations instead of stirring up trouble. I want to live a holy life. Part of a holy life includes showing the world Your love and hope, so I pray that I can do that by bringing peace to people's lives. In Your name I pray, amen.

INTENDED FOR GOOD

But Joseph said to them, "Don't be afraid. Am I in the place of God? You intended to harm me, but God intended it for good to accomplish what is now being done, the saving of many lives."

GENESIS 50:19–20 NIV

Father, I love the way You redeem what seems so hopeless in this world. You make things right that seem wrong. Just like the way You used Joseph's awful situation in Egypt to save so many people, You're also working things out for good in my life. When people may intend to harm me, You'll use those moments for good. You'll accomplish Your will in my life and in the world no matter what. For that, I'm grateful. And because of that, I can fall asleep in peace. In Jesus' name I pray, amen.

UNDER THE WEATHER

Is anyone among you sick? Let them call the elders of the church to pray over them and anoint them with oil in the name of the Lord. And the prayer offered in faith will make the sick person well; the Lord will raise them up. If they have sinned, they will be forgiven. Therefore confess your sins to each other and pray for each other so that you may be healed. The prayer of a righteous person is powerful and effective.

JAMES 5:14–16 NIV

Heavenly Father, You're the great Physician and Healer. As much as I know all of these truths, I'm still worried about my loved one who is so sick. I pray that You will comfort and help the person I love. I pray my loved one will come to know You better. You know if You have plans for healing here on earth or not—so I pray You'll give grace and peace to walk through this sickness. Please ease my loved one's pain and worries. I also pray You'll help me to be an encouragement, and that I'll be able to help in any way. Through this situation, I'm thankful I can trust in You completely. In Jesus' name I pray, amen.

you DESERVE PRAiSE!

*Every day I will bless you and praise your name
forever and ever. Great is the LORD, and greatly
to be praised, and his greatness is unsearchable.*

PSALM 145:2–3 ESV

Lord God, You are great! You're so worthy of praise,
and I'll never know the extent of Your majesty and
greatness. Tonight, I bless You and praise Your name.
Thank You for all You've done in my life and heart
today. Even when I think of the challenges and disap-
pointments I faced, You were there. As I think about
the wonderful moments You brought into my life, You
were there. You are faithful. You are good. And I'm
thankful You've chosen me as Your daughter. When
I'm tempted to focus on myself or things of this world,
please shift my focus to You and Your greatness. In
Jesus' name I pray, amen.

TOMORROW'S A NEW DAY

Sing the praises of the LORD, you his faithful people; praise his holy name. For his anger lasts only a moment, but his favor lasts a lifetime; weeping may stay for the night, but rejoicing comes in the morning.

PSALM 30:4–5 NIV

Lord God, I praise You! You are holy. There is nothing else like You in all of creation. I thank You for Your love and Your favor. Both are undeserved. And I couldn't earn any of it on my own. But You've chosen me, and for that I'm grateful. Thank You for forgiving my sin and giving me the undeserved gift of Your grace. Even when I fall asleep sad or exhausted after a long, emotional day, I thank You that I can wake up tomorrow with a fresh start. I may feel heartbroken tonight, but tomorrow morning, You can fill me with joy again. I pray that I'll find my joy in You and not look for it in my circumstances. You are so very good to me. In Jesus' name I pray, amen.

THINGS OF THE WORLD

What I mean, brothers and sisters, is that the time is short. From now on. . .those who buy something, [should live] as if it were not theirs to keep; those who use the things of the world, as if not engrossed in them. For this world in its present form is passing away.

1 CORINTHIANS 7:29–31 NIV

Father, it's very easy for me to get distracted by the world and to let the things of the world consume my time, energy, and thoughts. I don't want that to be the case for me though. And I don't want to base my success on what the world views as success. Please help me keep my focus on You. I want to rest in the fact that I don't have to work for Your approval. When You see me, You see me forgiven and accepted through Jesus' sacrifice. I am so grateful for that! It's in Jesus' name I pray, amen.

GOOD VS. EVIL

For it is better, if it is God's will, to suffer for doing good than for doing evil.

1 PETER 3:17 NIV

Father God, I want to do Your will, no matter what. And even though I can feel so pressured by people around me, I want to please You more than anyone else. Would You please give me strength to follow Your commands and live like Your daughter? Please help me make the right decisions, instead of choosing sinful ones. Even if it means suffering in this world, please help me stand strong and do what's right in Your eyes. Even if people make fun of me, purposely overlook me because of my belief in You, or try to harm me, I pray You'll protect me and remind me that You are the One I want to please. You are the ultimate Judge. And You are the one true God. I love You and want to spend my life honoring You, no matter what. In Jesus' name I pray, amen.

ALL MY NEEDS

*And my God will supply all your needs according
to His riches in glory in Christ Jesus.*

PHILIPPIANS 4:19 NASB

Father God, right now I admit that I'm worried. I wonder what is coming next and how You'll provide for me. What will happen in school? What job should I have. . .and what job will I have someday? What will happen with my family? Who are my true friends? What will happen in my love life? For all of my questions and uncertainty, I praise You for being my Provider. You're my Jehovah-jireh—the God who supplies all my needs. More than anything, I want to rest in the truth that You will provide all my needs according to Your riches in glory in Christ Jesus. Help me remember that the riches of Your glory are truly amazing. Thank You for blessing me so richly—even with some of my wants. I'm glad I can trust in You. In Jesus' name I pray, amen.

MAKING THE MOST OF EVERY OPPORTUNITY

Be very careful, then, how you live—not as unwise but as wise, making the most of every opportunity, because the days are evil.

EPHESIANS 5:15–16 NIV

Lord Jesus, I want to be careful with the way I live. Because of this, it's important that I carefully make day-to-day decisions. Please help me live wisely. As hard as it may seem to realize, all of the little choices I make add up. Every day is filled with little opportunities to follow You, obey what You command, and show Your love to the world around me. Please help me be a good witness and example for You with the words I say, my attitudes, and the way I treat other people. Show me the opportunities You have opened to me—and help me boldly use them for You. Please help me bring Your love to those who need it the most. In Your name I pray, amen.

HUNGER AND THIRST NO MORE

Then Jesus declared, "I am the bread of life.
Whoever comes to me will never go hungry, and
whoever believes in me will never be thirsty."

JOHN 6:35 NIV

Lord Jesus, I am so glad You are the Bread of Life. Even though You spoke in figures of speech, I'm glad that You alone satisfy a hunger nothing else can. You meet all my needs not only physically but also spiritually, and for that I'm so thankful. I pray that I'll stop trying to find fulfillment and satisfaction in the things of this world. Instead, I want to live in the freedom that You've given me everything I need. I don't have to worry about this life or the one to come because life is found in You and You alone. I'm thankful for You and the way You satisfy my soul completely. In Your name I pray, amen.

PEACE WITH YOU

Therefore, since we have been justified through faith, we have peace with God through our Lord Jesus Christ.

ROMANS 5:1 NIV

Heavenly Father, I would love to experience peace here in my little corner of the world. And I would love to experience peace tonight. You want me to experience peace too! But it's impossible for me to have peace right here, right now unless I have peace in heaven—with You. Thank You for Jesus. I ask Him to save me and lead my life as Lord. Thank You that Jesus came to give peace—not as the world gives, but only as He could give. Peace that doesn't involve the absence of something bad, like fighting, but peace that means the presence of something really good. Through Jesus, I've gained a serene, peaceful heart that I don't have to work for or earn. Thank You for Your peace that satisfies more than anything this world offers. In Jesus' name I pray, amen.

WHAT CAN COMPARE?

You have multiplied, O LORD my God, your
wondrous deeds and your thoughts toward us;
none can compare with you! I will proclaim and
tell of them, yet they are more than can be told.

PSALM 40:5 ESV

Father, I'm amazed by You. You created absolutely everything. Everything that has breath lives because of You. You know all. You have a perfect plan for everything—even if I don't understand what that plan is. But I don't have to understand to worship You and praise You for all You do. I praise You and You alone. Nothing and no one in this world compares to You. Your power is mind-boggling. The mercy You've shown me is undeserved and so kind. Thank You! I pray that I'll naturally tell people about You and the good things You've done for me. In Jesus' name I pray, amen.

ALL I NEED TO DO IS ASK

If any of you lacks wisdom, you should ask God, who gives generously to all without finding fault, and it will be given to you.

JAMES 1:5 NIV

Father God, sometimes I'm so confused. I just don't know what to do—on a normal day and especially when it comes to future plans. So much is uncertain. I don't know what Your will is for me and my life. I pray for wisdom! Please give me clear thoughts and help me make decisions wisely. I want to honor You with my choices. Thank You for giving generously in everything, but especially when it comes to wisdom. I pray You'll guide me and that I'll listen when You nudge me. As I look to You and Your Word, please help wise choices be obvious. And I pray my soul will rest as I trust You to lead me. In Jesus' name I pray, amen.

THE TREASURE OF WISDOM

How much better to get wisdom than gold! To get understanding is to be chosen rather than silver.
PROVERBS 16:16 ESV

Father, You know that it's easy for people to focus on money and belongings. According to Your Word, it's always been that way, but it seems like even more, people today really obsess over their possessions. I don't want to fall into that trap. When friends seem to get the newest and best of everything, I pray I wouldn't even want to keep up with them. Please help me remember that certain things are better than riches—like wisdom and understanding. I pray that instead of questing over money, I'll make wisdom my goal. Please help me understand the difference between right and wrong. And please help me figure out deeper meanings and consequences to decisions I make. Fill me with Your wisdom and understanding. Since I won't suddenly become wise overnight, please help me make wise decisions every day until I have a much better understanding of life. In Jesus' name I pray, amen.

MY HIDING PLACE

You are my hiding place; you will
protect me from trouble.

PSALM 32:7 NIV

Father God, I love that I can hide myself in You.
When bad things are happening all around me, I
can find shelter in You. You protect me from trouble
like nothing or no one else. And even if and when
I'm hurt, You're still a strong and sure place for me.
I'm glad I can run to You. I trust that You'll teach me
the way I should go and gently counsel me with love.
Thank You that You are for me and not against me.
In Jesus' name I pray, amen.

LIVING IN AN UNBELIEVING WORLD

*If you are insulted because of the name
of Christ, you are blessed, for the Spirit
of glory and of God rests on you.*

1 PETER 4:14 NIV

Lord God, You know what kind of pressures I face every day. You know how people in this world hate You and say absolutely horrid things about You. Comments that I hear about You and Your believers make me feel sick to my stomach. These ugly words only show what's inside of people's hearts—people who desperately need You to save them. Even when they say bad things about me because of You, I pray I'll remember it's actually a blessing. Every insult that comes from being Your follower only reminds me that I'm not of this world. There's more to this life. Thank You that Your Spirit of glory rests on me and makes me different from unbelievers. I pray I'll find my hope in You alone. In Jesus' name I pray, amen.

LiFE IS GOOD

*Surely your goodness and love will follow
me all the days of my life, and I will dwell
in the house of the LORD forever.*

PSALM 23:6 NIV

Lord, each and every day is a gift. I thank You for that but also realize that on bad days, it's hard to see Your gifts. Please open my eyes to all of the beauty around me—and all of the amazing things You're working out, whether I'm having a good or bad day. I know that regardless of what happens each day, Your goodness and love follow me. Wherever I go, whatever I do, You're surprising me with Your good gifts. Thank You! Thank You for adding joy to my life. And thank You that one day You'll welcome me into Your home to live with You forever. Surely that will be much more incredible than I can even imagine. I love You. In Jesus' name I pray, amen.

LiViNG LiKE I'M YOUNG

Flee the evil desires of youth and pursue
righteousness, faith, love and peace, along with
those who call on the Lord out of a pure heart.

2 TIMOTHY 2:22 NIV

Father, sometimes it feels like older people look down on teenagers. How many times have I heard, "Just wait until you grow up!"? I get tired of feeling like I'm less of a person because of my age. I know You value my life, and I know You have wonderful plans for me. But Your Word also clearly says that young people don't always make the wisest choices. If I'm supposed to flee the evil desires of youth, that means my heart will be pulled in a direction that doesn't bring You honor. If desires of young people can be evil, I pray You'd give me wisdom to know the difference between right and wrong. Even if it seems difficult or unpopular, please help me pursue righteousness, faith, love, and peace. Those things seem so different than what the world offers—and I pray I'd chase after them anyway. Please help me live a life of faith. I want to show Your love to the world around me. In Jesus' name I pray, amen.

THiNK ABOUT THiS...

Finally, brothers and sisters, whatever is true, whatever is noble, whatever is right, whatever is pure, whatever is lovely, whatever is admirable—if anything is excellent or praiseworthy—think about such things.

PHILIPPIANS 4:8 NIV

Lord, sometimes it's hard to think about good things. Surrounded by the muck of this world, it's hard to focus on what's true. Noble things seem hard to come by. The line between right and wrong seems blurry. Purity? It's like it's vanishing from the world around me. And things that are lovely, admirable, excellent, and praiseworthy can also be very hard to find. But I pray that I might find them in the everyday moments of life. Please help me delight in what's true, noble, right, pure, lovely, admirable, excellent, and praiseworthy. I'd love to be surprised by these things tomorrow—and celebrate them as wonderful gifts from You. In Jesus' name I pray, amen.

FAITH AND BELIEF

*This righteousness is given through
faith in Jesus Christ to all who believe.*

ROMANS 3:22 NIV

Father God, thank You for Jesus! Thank You that by
believing and having faith in Jesus Christ, I can be
made right with You. My faith in Jesus is a very real
thing I can possess or receive, a lot like I can receive
a present. When I'm given a gift, it's not truly mine
until I accept it and make it my own. I have to take it
from the giver and open it up. That's the same with
my faith. Jesus isn't truly mine until I accept Him and
make Him my own. I choose to do this with my mind
and my heart. And today, I choose to believe in Jesus
Christ and trust that Your righteousness will be given
to me through faith. In Jesus' name I pray, amen.

PEACEFUL SLEEP

In peace I will lie down and sleep, for you alone, LORD, make me dwell in safety.

PSALM 4:8 NIV

Heavenly Father, You are the God of peace. You've given me peace. And tonight, I can and will lie down and sleep in peace. I don't have to stay awake in fear because You're my great protector. I don't have to worry what might happen tomorrow because I know You'll prepare my way. I don't have to toss and turn all night because You make me dwell in safety. Your protection and safety and peace are such great gifts. Thank You! Thank You for freeing me so I don't have to feel like I'm a captive to fear. Thank You for the gift of sweet, peaceful sleep that restores my energy and revives my spirit. You are so good to me. In the name of Jesus, the Prince of Peace, I pray, amen.

NEVER FORGET

"Can a mother forget the baby at her breast and have no compassion on the child she has borne? Though she may forget, I will not forget you! See, I have engraved you on the palms of my hands."

ISAIAH 49:15–16 NIV

Lord Jesus, no matter what happens in my life, I always want to remember certain people. But as much as I know I want to remember people who are special to me, sometimes the human brain doesn't work as well as it should and people are forgotten. I thank You for never forgetting me. No matter what, You've promised to remember me—and when You look at Your nail-scarred hands, You're reminded of me. Knowing that I matter that much to You amazes me. Thank You for loving me and caring about me so very much. In Your name I pray, amen.

LISTEN AND DO

Do not merely listen to the word, and so deceive yourselves. Do what it says.
JAMES 1:22 NIV

Lord God, Your Word is true. It's living and active. It can judge my thoughts and my heart's intentions. It can guide me—if I'll let it. I thank You for the gift of Your Word. I pray I won't forget about it. I pray I won't just listen to it and then do my own thing. I want to do what Your Word asks. As it guides me, please give me strength and courage to follow what it says. I want what You say to direct my life. Please help me find what Your Word says, base my life on it, and put it into action—even if and when it seems difficult. In Jesus' name I pray, amen.

LAUGHiNG AT THE FUTURE

She is clothed with strength and dignity;
she can laugh at the days to come.

PROVERBS 31:25 NIV

Father, because I trust in You, I don't have to worry about my future. In fact, I can laugh at days that will come. When people around me are stressed out with what's going on in the world or are worried about what they should do, I can rest in You. You give me strength. And as I trust in You completely, You clothe me with dignity so that I'm worthy of honor and respect. Thank You! Knowing that I don't have to fear what's coming is huge. And feeling the strength You give me is such a comfort. You are so good to me, and I'm forever grateful. In Jesus' name I pray, amen.

PRAISE THE LORD!

I will bless the LORD at all times; his praise shall continually be in my mouth.

PSALM 34:1 ESV

Father God, I praise You! You created all things. You faithfully protect and provide for Your children. You have a plan for all of time and eternity. Nothing escapes Your notice, and nothing surprises You. Even when I feel like I don't have much faith, You are faithful. Even when I feel like I don't have much love, You are loving. Even when sin separated humans from Your perfection, You made a way of forgiveness and mercy through Jesus. Thank You! I needed to be saved. When it seems like everything goes wrong in my day, I can stop to praise You because You are good, even when my circumstances are not. And You will comfort and guide me even when times are tough. When I have an amazing day, I can stop to praise You because You give all good things. Your awesomeness is so much more than I can comprehend. In Jesus' name I pray, amen.

WHAT IS LOVE?

Love is patient and kind; love does not envy or boast; it is not arrogant or rude. It does not insist on its own way; it is not irritable or resentful; it does not rejoice at wrongdoing, but rejoices with the truth. Love bears all things, believes all things, hopes all things, endures all things. Love never ends.

1 CORINTHIANS 13:4–8 ESV

Father, Your love is patient and kind. It continues forever. It changes the world, and it has changed my heart and my life. When I think of Your love, my own love for others doesn't measure up. In fact, I feel so unloving in comparison to You. Jesus said people would know His followers by their love. And He demonstrated how to love others well. I want to be like Jesus. I want to love others exceptionally well—and I want to be known as a loving girl. Please fill me with Your Holy Spirit and let Your love spill out of me to all who are around me. In Jesus' name I pray, amen.

WHERE DOES MY HELP COME FROM?

I lift up my eyes to the mountains—where does my help come from? My help comes from the LORD, the Maker of heaven and earth. He will not let your foot slip—he who watches over you will not slumber.

PSALM 121:1–3 NIV

Lord, I need Your help. Right now, I want to quit. When life and circumstances are hard, it seems easier to give up and move on. But You never quit. And You never stop watching out for me. Thank You for Your nonstop, never-ending help! Thank You for protecting me. You never, ever sleep, so You're always aware of what's going on in my life and everywhere around the whole universe. I'm amazed how You've created everything—the mountains, the oceans, every single unique person, even heaven and all of earth. And even as You've made all of that and take care of it all, You still love and care for me. You are so worthy of all my honor and praise. I love You! In Jesus' name I pray, amen.

CONTENTMENT!

But godliness with contentment is great gain.
For we brought nothing into the world, and we
can take nothing out of it. But if we have food
and clothing, we will be content with that.

1 TIMOTHY 6:6–8 NIV

Father God, I pray I would be content with all You've given me. It's so easy to get caught up in thinking about what I wish I had and what I don't have. Why do I always seem to want more? Or something different? Please help me remember that I didn't bring a single thing with me into this world when I was born. And when I die, I won't take anything with me. Instead of thinking about things—clothes and belongings and what I want to eat—please help me focus on being more like You. When I'm more like You, I become more content. And when I become more like You, I can take that with me. In Jesus' name I pray, amen.

HONOR

*"Honor your father and mother"—which is
the first commandment with a promise—
"so that it may go well with you and that
you may enjoy long life on the earth."*
EPHESIANS 6:2–3 NIV

Father, sometimes I get so angry with my parents. I don't always understand why You chose this family for me. Even though I get frustrated at times, please help me see the ways they're a blessing to me. I pray that they might understand me and where I'm coming from—and that I might, in some way, understand them and where they're coming from too. I know You want me to honor them. And I know I should. So even when I don't feel like doing that, please help me. Please help me appreciate what they're doing, and help me learn from them. In Jesus' name I pray, amen.

FEARLESS

*"So have no fear of them, for nothing is covered
that will not be revealed, or hidden that will not
be known. What I tell you in the dark, say in the
light, and what you hear whispered, proclaim
on the housetops. And do not fear those who
kill the body but cannot kill the soul."*

<small>MATTHEW 10:26–28 ESV</small>

Lord Jesus, when You lived on earth, You knew what
was in the heart of men. Yet You knew You didn't
have to fear men. You didn't fear what they thought
of You or what they would do to You. You, as the
Son of God, knew that even if men could kill Your
body, they couldn't ever kill Your soul. I'm thankful
You didn't live in fear—and because of You and Your
sacrifice for me, I don't have to live in fear either.
Please help me boldly live for You. Please use my
mouth, my mind, and my hands to help point others
to You. Please help me proclaim Your truth and Your
teachings to the world around me without fear. In
Your name I pray, amen.

I'M YOUR GIRL

The LORD called me from the womb, from the
body of my mother he named my name.

ISAIAH 49:1 ESV

Lord God, You know I'm Your girl. You've known me since before I was created. You know I'm wonderfully made. You called me from my mother's womb. You chose me and delight in me. This is so amazing to think about! Sometimes I wonder exactly why. Why me? I'll never know the answer, but You do. Thank You. Thank You for calling me. Thank You for naming me. Thank You for choosing me as Your own. It's so incredible, and I'm forever grateful. In Jesus' name I pray, amen.

VANISHED!

*As far as the east is from the west, so far
does he remove our transgressions from us.*
PSALM 103:12 ESV

Lord, You know my sins. Tonight I come to You and confess what I've done. Instead of living with the burden of all I've done wrong, please help me accept Your forgiveness. Knowing that You completely remove my sins astounds me. They've vanished. You've removed them as far as the east is from the west—and that is so far! Thank You for Your forgiveness. Please help me turn from my sin and walk the other way. Through Your Holy Spirit, please help me live in obedience to You. I want to please You and represent You in everything I say and do. In Jesus' name I pray, amen.

DOING WHAT'S RIGHT

For what credit is there if, when you sin and are
harshly treated, you endure it with patience? But
if when you do what is right and suffer for it you
patiently endure it, this finds favor with God.

1 PETER 2:20 NASB

Father God, it's hard to make decisions between right and wrong every single day. I just wish right choices would already be made for me! But life in this world is not like that. I pray You'll help me know what's right to do—and then do it. And I want to do what's right, no matter what. Even if people make fun of me or threaten to do things to me, even if people make my life miserable, I still want to do what is right. I need Your help to do this. I know it will be hard but so worth it—and I know it's what You want me to do. In Jesus' name I pray, amen.

WAITING FOR YOU

I waited patiently for the LORD;
he turned to me and heard my cry.

PSALM 40:1 NIV

Father, thank You for hearing my prayers. Thank You for being worthy of being prayed to. I love that I can trust You. And I love that You have planned what's best for me. I want to be honest though. I've been praying about something for a long time. You know what it is. I keep praying because this is important to me. Please help me be patient as I wait for You and Your answer. I know Your answer might be yes—or it might be no. Or it might be to wait. Oh, the waiting is hard! But no matter what Your answer is and especially in the waiting, I choose to put all of my trust in You. I love You! In Jesus' name I pray, amen.

WE ARE FAMILY

But to all who did receive him, who believed in his name, he gave the right to become children of God, who were born, not of blood nor of the will of the flesh nor of the will of man, but of God.
JOHN 1:12–13 ESV

Father God, I am so thankful You've given people the right to become Your children. Even though not everyone accepts that right, You've still invited everyone. I'll gladly take Your invitation. I receive Christ and believe in His name. And as I do that, I'm thankful that I'm born of You—as Your child. Your daughter. It wasn't anything my body willed. It didn't depend on my family. It hasn't depended on my actions. It's Your will, and Yours alone. And it's Your amazing gift to me. Thank You! I am glad I'm part of Your family. In Jesus' name I pray, amen.

BE CHOOSY

My dear brothers and sisters, take note of this:
Everyone should be quick to listen, slow to speak and
slow to become angry, because human anger does
not produce the righteousness that God desires.

JAMES 1:19-20 NIV

Lord Jesus, please watch over my mouth. It's so easy to blurt out what I'm thinking. Or even worse, it's easy to just start talking without thinking about what I'm saying. It can be embarrassing to realize what I've said simply because I haven't thought about the words I've chosen. Please help me be a better listener—and quick to listen instead of thinking about what I want to say in response. I pray that as I listen, I wouldn't make quick judgments or reactions. Please help me be slow when it comes to getting angry. Please help me keep my tongue and emotions in check. It's hard, but through You and Your power, I know it's possible. In Your name I pray, amen.

THE AUTHOR OF MY STORY

Your eyes have seen my unformed substance;
and in Your book were all written the days
that were ordained for me, when as yet
there was not one of them.

PSALM 139:16 NASB

Father God, You are amazing. You have created all things, including me. And You know all things, including every single moment of my life. You've written the story of my life, one day at a time. And even though certain moments don't always make sense, they all tie together into a beautiful life. You've known me since before my mother knew me. No detail of my life has escaped Your notice. As much as I'd like to know what's in store for me or why certain things have happened—or not happened—I choose to trust in You as the Master Storyteller. Thank You that You have a plan for me. And thank You for knowing everything about me and choosing to love me in spite of all my weaknesses. In Jesus' name I pray, amen.

FOCUS ON THE GOOD

Rejoice always, pray without ceasing,
give thanks in all circumstances; for this
is the will of God in Christ Jesus for you.
1 Thessalonians 5:16–18 ESV

Father God, I love that Your will for me is to rejoice! And to pray to You. And to thank You for everything. What a wonderful will for my life. This world is so negative and can drag me down easily. But You never intended that for me. You intend to bring life. And You want me to live a life that overflows with joy. When I have bad days, I pray I'll turn to You in prayer. Even when it feels like things are crumbling around me, I pray I'll be able to find something that's worth thanking You for and something I can rejoice over. Please help me focus on the wonderful things that are happening even right now and experience the true freedom that comes through You. In Jesus' name I pray, amen.

FORGETTING WHAT'S BEHIND

*Brothers, I do not consider that I have made it
my own. But one thing I do: forgetting what lies
behind and straining forward to what lies ahead,
I press on toward the goal for the prize of the
upward call of God in Christ Jesus.*

PHILIPPIANS 3:13–14 ESV

Lord Jesus, You've promised me such a prize. As I've
trusted You with my life and believe that You are my
living Savior, You've promised me an eternity with
You! A reward instead of punishment. Life with You
instead of separation. A transformed heart and soul.
I pray that I'll forget about the things of this world. I
pray I won't get bogged down with everyday matters.
And I pray I'll forget my past. Instead, I want to press
on to live in Your freedom. You've called me to an
amazing prize—I pray I might strain toward that every
day, remembering You're my Lord and that You've
called me as Your own. In Your name I pray, amen.

ALL I NEED

*Whom have I in heaven but you? And there
is nothing on earth that I desire besides you.
My flesh and my heart may fail, but God is the
strength of my heart and my portion forever.*

PSALM 73:25–26 ESV

Father God, You are all I want. There's nothing else
on this earth I truly desire except for You. Everyday
things and people try to rob my attention and affection from You, but at my very heart, I know nothing
else can compare to You. Not any other relationship.
Not any belonging or possession. Not any award or
honor or opportunity. You and You alone are the true
strength of my heart. Everything and everyone else
might fall away, but I'll still have You. Please help
me live like that every day. Please keep my focus on
You and not on the stuff of this world. Thank You for
being my one true, steady, never-failing Rock who I
can base my life, future, and eternity on. In Jesus'
name I pray, amen.

SO MUCH LIFE

*"I came that they may have life,
and have it abundantly."*

JOHN 10:10 NASB

Father, You are the giver of all life. You are the Creator of life, and Jesus came so that I might live an overflowing life of plenty. A lot of days my life doesn't feel so abundant though. It's really easy to get discouraged, and sometimes I don't even know if I want to live to see the future. I pray that You would open my eyes to see the gift of life. Please help me see how important I am in the lives of other people. And please, even (and especially) when I'm feeling down, show me how I can use my life for You. I pray You would protect me from Satan's schemes to steal, kill, and destroy. Please help me live for You! In Jesus' name I pray, amen.

LiSTEN

The Lord GOD has given me the tongue of
those who are taught, that I may know how
to sustain with a word him who is weary.
Morning by morning he awakens; he awakens
my ear to hear as those who are taught.

ISAIAH 50:4 ESV

Lord God, I want You to lead me. And I want to follow Your lead. Sometimes, though, I just don't know what You'd like from me. Tomorrow morning, could You please wake me up so I can hear You? Please help my ear focus on You and Your truth. When I'm feeling weary with all of the things I need to do, please refresh me. I want to learn to rest in You and listen to You throughout my day. As I pray tonight, I believe You will reveal Your will and Word to me. I believe You can revive me in the middle of my tiredness. Thank You for always being there for me and always being willing to guide me. In Jesus' name I pray, amen.

GREAT THiNGS

The LORD has done great things
for us, and we are filled with joy.
PSALM 126:3 NIV

Lord, You have done great things for me! You've chosen me. You've called me Your own. You've opened my eyes and heart to Your truth. You've rescued me through Christ. All of those great things fill me with joy. They give me hope and a future. They comfort me when life feels overwhelming. I thank You that I can trust You completely—moment by moment and with my entire future. Joy is an incredible gift that comes from You. Thank You for the way it fills my soul and overflows to every part of my life. I pray it would be contagious to the people around me, and I pray I would tell about the great things You have done. In Jesus' name I pray, amen.

WHAT CAN HAPPEN?

In God I trust and am not afraid.
What can man do to me?
PSALM 56:11 NIV

Father, I'm glad I can come to You with anything. And tonight I admit that sometimes I get scared about what's happening in the world. I know You didn't create mankind to live this way—everything changed once sin entered the picture in the Garden of Eden. But it's good to know that even if and when people intend to harm others, Your purposes and plans will stand. Your name is a strong tower for those who trust You—and I trust You! When I run to Your name, I am safe. Please help me bravely shine Your light in this dark world. Please help me change my corner of the world with Your love. Please help me boldly stand for You. In Jesus' name I pray, amen.

WHAT IS BEAUTIFUL?

Charm is deceptive, and beauty is fleeting;
but a woman who fears the LORD is to be praised.

PROVERBS 31:30 NIV

Lord, every day I face messages about beauty. What is attractive? Am I beautiful enough? How can I change my beauty—or lack of beauty? It's frustrating and even at times heartbreaking. I want to be beautiful, but I'm just me. Please help me remember that you don't see beauty the same way humans do. You look at the heart, not at appearances. And what is beautiful in the heart is someone who fears You. Please help me become ravishingly beautiful on the inside. Please help my love for You and faith in You glow and shine to others around me. May the beauty of my relationship with You be captivating and long-lasting instead of fleeting like external beauty. In Your name I pray, amen.

WATCHFUL PROTECTION

The Lᴏʀᴅ watches over you—the Lᴏʀᴅ is your shade at your right hand; the sun will not harm you by day, nor the moon by night.

PSALM 121:5-6 NIV

Lord God, You are so good to me. With You, I don't have to fear. Thank You for watching over me all day and all night long. I don't have to worry about harm—not in the light of day and not in the dark of night. I don't have to worry about getting scorched by things of this world—You're my shade! Please continue to watch over me, especially when I'm scared by what people try to do to me. Please protect me from evil plans. When I'm wronged, I turn to You for help. Please continue to keep me safe. In Jesus' name I pray, amen.

ABOVE ALL, LOVE

Above all, love each other deeply, because love covers over a multitude of sins.

1 PETER 4:8 NIV

Lord Jesus, thank You for living a life of love here on earth. You loved people so deeply, and You were the perfect model of how we should be known by our love. Sometimes I don't feel very loving. But I pray I'd love people anyway. Please help me to love others sincerely, just like You loved. Please help me love those who seem unlovable—and even people who don't seem to deserve my love. I need to remember that I don't always act lovable, and I don't deserve Your love. But You love me anyway. And Your love has changed my life and my future. Thank You for covering over my sins with Your love. I pray my life would reflect Your love and make it obvious that I am Yours. In Your name I pray, amen.

DARK IS LIGHT

*If I say, "Surely the darkness will hide me and the
light become night around me," even the darkness
will not be dark to you; the night will shine like
the day, for darkness is as light to you.*

PSALM 139:11–12 NIV

Lord God, I love that since You created this world,
nothing about it is above or beyond You. You created the light and the darkness. So even though it
might seem like darkness is so overwhelming—and so
dark—to me, it's not dark to You. As much as I can't
understand it, darkness is like light to You. The night
shines like day. Because of that, I can fall asleep
tonight in peace. I don't have to fear what I can't see
in the darkness because You can see everything, and
You're right here to protect me. I pray that tonight
my body, my mind, and my soul will find rest in You.
As I wake up tomorrow morning well rested, I pray
I'll be ready to praise and serve You! In Jesus' name
I pray, amen.

ARMOR UP!

Finally, be strong in the Lord and in the strength
of His might. Put on the full armor of God,
so that you will be able to stand firm
against the schemes of the devil.

EPHESIANS 6:10–11 NASB

Lord, I want to be strong in You. Sometimes I feel like I'm so weak. But I don't want my weakness to be used against me—or as a reason to sin. I want to stand firm against the devil's schemes. I want to experience the strength of Your might. Please help me put on—and keep on—Your armor: The belt of truth that keeps all my defenses firmly in place. The breastplate of righteousness that protects my heart. Readiness and preparation given by the Gospel of peace that guards me like protective shoes. The shield of faith that helps me extinguish the fiery darts Satan uses to harm me. The helmet of salvation to guard my thinking. The sword of the Spirit—Your Word!—that is my powerful defense. Thank You for that powerful armor that can withstand all. In Jesus' name I pray, amen.

THE HOPE OF GLORY

*To them God chose to make known how
great among the Gentiles are the riches
of the glory of this mystery, which is
Christ in you, the hope of glory.*

COLOSSIANS 1:27 ESV

Father God, realizing that You chose to make Yourself
known to me in the most intimate way—Christ in me—
is almost too much to grasp. But once Jesus Christ
became my Lord and Savior, He began living in me.
That's mysterious and mind-blowing and marvelous.
He's not distant. Christ living inside of me is the hope
of glory. Centuries before Christ even was born, You
promised You would send hope and help to people,
and You did. And centuries later when You chose me
and chose to make Christ known to me, You blessed
me with an amazing gift and amazing hope. Thank
You! I pray I'll live a changed life knowing this hope of
glory. And I pray I'll live worthy of all the riches You've
so generously given me. In Jesus' name I pray, amen.

YOU ARE GREAT!

*But may all who seek you rejoice and be glad
in you; may those who long for your saving
help always say, "The LORD is great!"*

PSALM 40:16 NIV

Lord, You are great! And I rejoice in You. It's an amazing thing to know You and be known by You. You make me glad—from the tips of my toes to the top of my head. Sometimes my heart feels like it could burst with Your joy. Thank You for Your saving help. Thank You that I'm never alone. Please help me to remember that all I need to do is seek You and You'll be found. I pray that tomorrow I'll think about Your greatness all day long and that it will change the way I live. I love You! In Jesus' name I pray, amen.

NEVER LEFT ALONE

*Keep your life free from love of money, and be
content with what you have, for he has said,
"I will never leave you nor forsake you."*

HEBREWS 13:5 ESV

Lord, thank you for keeping Your promises. I know when You promise that You will never leave me nor forsake me, it's true. I'm so glad that You won't. It's comforting to know I'm never truly alone. Sometimes, though, it's hard to imagine You never, ever leaving me—not even for a split second. But a promise is a promise, and You always keep Your promises. Please help me be content with what You give me. Even when I think I know what I want—or when I want something different than You give—please help me not be ungrateful. Thank You for what I have. Thank You that I don't have to chase after the things of this world; I need only chase after You. In Jesus' name I pray, amen.

BURDEN SHARER

Praise be to the Lord, to God our Savior,
who daily bears our burdens.

PSALM 68:19 NIV

Lord, You are my God and Savior, and I praise You. I also thank You that I'm not alone in this life—You share it with me. And every day, You bear my burdens. Even when I'm feeling burdened, You pick up my burdens and carry them for me. You don't leave me to struggle with them on my own. It's a relief to know You're with me and that You shoulder what's weighing me down. Jesus promised that if I would just come to Him, I'd find rest. I do come to Him! His yoke is easy and His burden is light. I pray that I'll continue to find freedom, relief, and rest in Him. Thank You for releasing me from the weight of this world. I love finding freedom and peace in You. In Jesus' name I pray, amen.

HARD TO BE HUMBLE

Humble yourselves before the Lord,
and he will lift you up.
JAMES 4:10 NIV

Father, tonight I come to You humbled. It's not easy to lower myself—so often it's easier to think well of myself and puff myself up. But I want to take my eyes off of myself. I want to stop thinking so highly of myself and realize exactly what I am: a girl who desperately needs her Lord. Father, I pray that I'll remember who I am and who You are. You are in control of everything, and I'm not. You're so loving and just and filled with mercy. If I'm honest with myself, I struggle every day. I want to be more loving. I want to be more just and merciful to others. But it's so hard. And it's hard to be humble. I pray I might remember what I deserve—separation from You— and how Jesus has saved me from my fate. Thank You for His gift. In Jesus' name I pray, amen.

I NEED YOU

Hear my prayer, LORD; let my cry for help come to you. Do not hide your face from me when I am in distress. Turn your ear to me; when I call, answer me quickly.

PSALM 102:1–2 NIV

Lord, I need You! Things in my life feel like they're too much for me to handle on my own. I'm nervous, anxious, and a little scared. I know You can help me and that You'll never leave me or abandon me. Please help me rest in that. When it feels like my life has spun out of control and I have little hope, I want to remember You. You're compassionate and full of love. You listen to the cries of my heart. You care about how I'm feeling right now. And You know me. I pray You'll fill me with Your peace and help me know that You've heard my cries for help. In Jesus' name I pray, amen.

Yours

But if we walk in the Light as He Himself is in the Light, we have fellowship with one another, and the blood of Jesus His Son cleanses us from all sin.

1 JOHN 1:7 NASB

Lord Jesus, thank You for cleansing me from my sin with Your blood. You know how I've sinned against You. And I'm sorry, Lord. I gladly accept Your forgiveness and pray that I could live a changed life. The Father sees me through You now—not through my own weaknesses and wrongs. I pray I'll walk in Your light and not the darkness of this world. Please help me live a life worthy of You. And please help me be a light to the world, showing others Your truth. I pray my life will look different than the lives of other people around me, so that it's obvious I'm Yours. Not my own. Not anyone else's. But Yours. In Your name I pray, amen.

WHAT'S MY PURPOSE?

The LORD will fulfill his purpose for me; your
steadfast love, O LORD, endures forever.
Do not forsake the work of your hands.

PSALM 138:8 ESV

Lord, so often I wonder what I should do with my life. What have I been created for? Why am I here? Why did You put me right here, right now? Even though I have a zillion questions, You have a zillion answers. You know why I'm here. You know what I've been created for. You know Your purpose for me—and You know how I can fulfill that. I pray I would follow Your leading, Lord. I pray You'll reveal Your purpose for me and confirm it in the circumstances of my life. Thank You for loving me with an enduring love. Thank You for creating me with a specific purpose. This is both huge to try to comprehend and so exciting! In Jesus' name I pray, amen.

EVERY SPIRITUAL BLESSING

Praise be to the God and Father of our Lord Jesus Christ, who has blessed us in the heavenly realms with every spiritual blessing in Christ.

EPHESIANS 1:3 NIV

God and Father of my Lord Jesus Christ, I praise You! You are holy. You are powerful. You have an amazing plan. And You have chosen to bless me with so much more than I can ever imagine or deserve. To realize that my blessings are in the heavenly realms is something I can't wrap my brain around. And the fact that You've blessed me with every spiritual blessing in Christ? Wow! I pray I will celebrate and rest in these truths when I'm tempted to feel bogged down by the stuff of this life. Thank You for Your incredible gifts. In my Lord Jesus Christ's name I pray, amen.